Endorsements for

Understanding Cults the Basics:
A Foundational Course for Clinicians

During this time of cultural instability and growing distrust of institutions, increasing numbers of people are coming under the influence of coercively controlling malignant narcissistic individuals and cultic groups, all too frequently at enormous emotional and financial costs. Dr. Steven Hassan's excellent 9-module course, Understanding Cults: A Foundational Course for Clinicians, provides critical information for physicians, psychotherapists, attorneys, family members, and the loved ones of those individuals who have been or are in such relationships. Comprehensive and thorough, here is where you will receive critical information about how to recognize these relationships, what to do, how to help, and most importantly, how to recover. Often missed and not recognized by professionals, and a common reason why treatment fails or remains incomplete, this fills a huge gap in the training of professionals and the kind of assistance needed for those who are affected.
    Jeffrey D. Rediger, MD, MDiv, Harvard Medical School, Author of *CURED*

"As a medical doctor with decades of experience, I wish to say that I very much enjoyed the content, and I think it is incredibly well done.
The course is highly comprehensive, and I believe anyone taking all the modules will come out with a very good understanding of this topic.
If everyone took this course and absorbed the messages, the world would be a much safer and more loving place for all."
    Richard Parker, MD

Outstanding - necessary for all mental health practitioners!

This was probably the best organized asynchronous course I've ever taken. Dr. Hassan is thorough, and leads learners step by step to understanding undue interpersonal and cultural influences, which can be seen in politics, mass psychology, and affecting now 10s of millions of people. I've always hoped for a plan to help deal with the fallout from our culture's tilt at abusive power - this course can be part of that plan. Essential!
    Ravi Chandra

Understanding Cults:
A Foundational Course

Steven Hassan, PhD

Freedom of Mind Press
Northampton, MA
2025

A Freedom of Mind Press Book

ISBN: 978-0-9670688-7-9

Library of Congress Control Number: 2025904959

Hassan, Steven
Understanding Cults: A Foundational Course
Workbook

1. Psychology 2. Cults 3. Recovery
4. Brainwashing 5. Deprogramming

Readers can reach Steven Hassan or The Freedom of Mind Resource Center Inc. at
www.freedomofmind.com

Accompanying course for
clinicians (CE/CME)

Accompanying General
Interest Courses

Contents

Introduction Xi

Module 1: Understanding Cult Mind Control   1
Utilize A Biopsychosocial Framework 2
Types Of Cults   2
Mind Control And The DSM-V-TR   4
Case Study — Laura 5
Healthy And Unhealthy Social Influence   8
The Influence Continuum — Individuals   8
The Influence Continuum — Leaders   10
The Influence Continuum — Organizations 10
The BITE Model   12
Symptoms Of Undue Influence   13
Is Your Client Under Mind Control?   17
Assessment   18
Clients May Not Realize They Are Under Mind Control   18
Set Your Goals   19
Conclusion   20

Module 2: Vulnerability And Recruitment 22
The Fundamental Attribution Error   23
Vulnerabilities To Cult Recruitment   27
Situational Vulnerabilities   28
Individual Vulnerabilities   28
Recruitment Strategies   35
In-Person Recruitment   35
Online Recruitment   37
The Victim Becomes The Victimizer 38

Module 3: Examining Destructive Cults   43
The Pyramid Structure Of Destructive Cults 45
Types Of Cults   46
Political Cults 46
Religious/Spiritual Cults   48
Self-Help Or Pseudo-Therapy Cults 48
Large Group Awareness Training   49
Multi-Level Marketing Cults 52
Human Trafficking   52
Mini-Cults   54

Family Cults   54
One-On-One Cults   55
Conspiracy Theory Cults   56
Clinicians Are Not Immune   59
The Profile Of A Cult Leader: Malignant Narcissism 59
Case Study: Marshall Applewhite/ Heaven's Gate   61
Cult Leader Examples   64
Charles Manson   64
Jim Jones   64
David Koresh 64
Bhagwan Shree Rajneesh   65
Ron Hubbard 65
Tony Alamo   66
Keith Raniere 66
Michael W. Fine   66

Module 4: Influence And Control   71

The Influence Continuum   74
Individuals   74
Leaders   75
Organizations 75
Undue Influence   76
Due Influence Vs. Undue Influence   77
Alan Scheflin's Social Influence Model (SIM)78
Subtle Vs. Extreme Undue Influence 82
Mind Control Vs. Brainwashing   83
Benign Cults Vs. Harmful Cults   84
Case Study: Patricia Hearst   87
How Does Undue Influence Happen?   89
Hypnosis   90
My Pathway Into Hypnosis 91
Hypnosis In Mind Control Cults   92
Protecting Yourself And Others From Unethical Hypnosis   94
DSM-V-TR Classification   97

Module 5: Theories And Models Of Mind Control 100

Cognitive Dissonance Theory
Social Psychologist Leon Festinger   101
Robert Jay Lifton's Thought Reform Model   102
1. Milieu Control   103
2. Mystical Manipulation   103
3. Demand For Purity 104

4. The Cult Of Confession   104
5. Sacred Science   104
6. Loading The Language   105
7. Doctrine Over Person   105
8. Dispensing Of Existence   106
Margaret Singer's 6 Conditions For Thought Reform   107
Hassan's BITE Model Of Mind Control   110
Behavior Control   111
Information Control   111
Thought Control   113
Emotion Control   114

Module 6: Cult Psychology 119
The Doctrine Is Reality   120
Reality Is All Or Nothing, Us Vs. Them, Good Vs. Evil   121
Elitist Mentality   123
Group Will Over Individual Will   124
Strict Obedience: Modeling The Leader   124
Happiness Through Good Performance   125
Manipulation Through Fear And Guilt 127
Emotional Highs And Lows   127
Changes In Time Orientation 128
No Way Out   129
Selective Recruitment 131
Illusion Of Choice   131

Module 7: Identity Change 134
Born Or Raised In A Cult   135
Client Intake For People Raised In A Cult   136
Reclaiming The Authentic Self   138
Case Study — Frances Peters   138
Client Intake For People Recruited Into A Cult   143
Three Stages Of Gaining Control Of The Mind   143
1. Unfreezing 144
Disorientation And Confusion 144
Sensory Deprivation And Overload   145
Psychological Manipulation   145
Hypnosis   145
Getting The Person To Question Self-Identity   146
Redefining The Individual's Past   146
Use Of Drugs And Alcohol   146
2. Changing   146

Formal And Informal Indoctrination Sessions 147
Reward And Punishment   147
Mystical Manipulation 147
Hypnosis And Mind-Altering Techniques   147
Confession And Testimonials 148
3. Refreezing 148
The Dual Identity Model   151
Conflict Between The Authentic Self And The Cult Self   151
The Authentic Self Survives   151

Module 8: How To Help: Psychoeducation
Empowering People To Become Their Authentic Self   155
Client-Centered Psychotherapy   155
A Specialized Approach: Assessment And Treatment Steps 157
Therapeutic Considerations   158
Is The Client Safe?   158
Are They Still In Contact With The Cult In Any Way?   158
Do They Have Their Basic Needs Met?   159
Are They Still Doing Cult Practices? 159
Assessing Past Traumas   159
Psychoeducation   160
Teaching About What Is Safe, Normal, And Healthy 160
What Does A Healthy Childhood Look Like? 160
Home Education Vs. Public Education   160
Exposure To The Internet And Social Media 161
Child Abuse   161
Attachment Style   161
Parental Alienation   161
Critical Thinking, Gut Feeling, Inner Voice   162
Focus On The Present   162
Some Additional Considerations   163
Clinical Qualities   166
Curiosity   166
Empathy   166
Attuned Listening Skills   167
Hopeful Outlook   167
Knowing When To Share Personal Information   167
Discriminate False Vs. True Memories   167
Non-Judgment   168

Module 9: Strategies & Techniques For Working With Former Cult Members 171
Insights For Working With This Population   171
Therapeutic Tools   174
Associated Vs. Dissociated Memory 174
Narrative Therapeutic Approaches   175
Create New Support Systems   175
Teach Paying Attention To One's Needs First   176
Therapeutic Techniques   178
Life Is A Journey; There Is No "One" Static "You."   179
Orientation Towards Learning And Growth Vs. Perfectionism   179
People Have Five Or More Careers Throughout Their Lifetime   180
Focus On Skills And Strategies   180
Evolve From Simplistic Binary Childish Thinking   180
Neurodiversity — Start With Strengths And Interests   180
Jagged Profile: Neurodiversity Including Asd, Adhd, Dyslexia   181
Intensive In-Person Sessions 181
Identifying And Undoing Triggers   182
Caution On Group Therapy   183
Cautions For Therapeutic Intervention   184
The Power Of Language   186
Healing Goals 189
Cultivating An Internal Locus Of Control   189
Being In The "Here And Now" 189
Toolbox Of Strategies And Techniques For Reality-Testing 190
Decision-Making Strategies   190
Trusting Oneself And Evaluating When To Trust Others   190
Reflect On The Knowledge They Have Now That They Didn't Have Before   191
Education On Neuroplasticity And Neurogenesis   191
Spirituality — What Is The Purpose Of Life? 191
Post-Traumatic Stress Disorder (PTSD)   192
The Role Of Family And Friends   193
Strategic Interactive Approach (SIA) 193
Hypothetical Questions   194
"What If God Wants You To Leave?" 194
"What If The Leader Admits He Is Not The Messiah (Prophet, Apostle, Avatar, Enlightened Master)?"   196
"Would You Kill Yourself (Or Someone Else) If The Leader Asked You To?"   196
"What If You Don't Earn The Money The Recruiter Promised?"   196
Strategies For Healing   197
Three-Step Phobia Cure   198
Step One: Phobia Vs. Legitimate Fear   199
Step Two: Explaining How Other Groups Use Phobias   199

Step Three: Discussing Specifics Of Their Situation 199
Approaches For Interaction   202
Approach Their Cult Involvement Indirectly   202
Ask About Key Experiences Pivotal To Their Commitment   203
Ask Them To Describe Moments Of Doubt   203
Connect The Person Back To Their Authentic Self   203
Expressive Therapies 203
Common Autism Spectrum Disorder (ASD) Challenges That May Be Exploited   204

Steven Hassan's Books   206

Conclusion   206

About The Author   209

INTRODUCTION

Welcome!

I am very excited to share my foundational course with you. This course has taken years to assemble with the help of social worker and college lecturer Phoebe Cellitti. I wanted to create an online course to help train and support mental health professionals working with clients who have suffered from all types of authoritarian mind control.

This course is the first of its kind. It has been designed by me, someone who was deprogrammed from the Moon cult, became a deprogrammer, then an exit-counselor, and then a trained mental health professional whose focus has been working with this population since 1976.

That said, it is for anyone concerned about harmful influence in cases of destructive religious and political cults, human trafficking, extremist and terrorist groups, one-on-one relationships, families, parental alienation, mini-cults, therapy and self-improvement groups, professional and institutional abuse, corporate and multi-level marketing programs, and harmful belief systems.

The course will benefit clinicians due to the ethical requirement for mental health professionals to only work with clients they are trained to treat. However, it will also be valuable for anyone seeking insight into cult mind control. Whether you have personally experienced cult involvement or have a loved one in a cult, you will benefit from exploring cult psychology and recovery.

I felt "called" to this work after being deprogrammed from the Moon cult in 1976. I was shocked, ashamed, and embarrassed when I realized my mind had been hacked. I was shocked by the fact that my values, integrity, and personality had been compromised. Unfortunately, at the time, there were limited resources available for recovery. So, over the last 48 years, I've dedicated myself to helping individuals to be empowered to reality-test and hopefully exit destructive cults and controlling relationships.

I wrote my first book, *Combating Cult Mind Control: The #1 Best-Selling Guide to Protection, Rescue, and Recovery from Destructive Cults,* in 1988. It was published in 10 languages and is widely regarded as the best single book on the subject. This early edition was published with the UK spelling of two "t" s in Combatting.

In 2000, I published *Releasing the Bonds: Empowering People to Think for Themselves.* In 2012, I decided to take the key points from *Releasing the Bonds* and publish a paperback, *Freedom of Mind: Helping Loved Ones Leave Controlling People, Cults and Beliefs.* This book was intended to be read after reading the new *Combating Cult Mind*

Control. It explains my Strategic Interactive Approach (SIA) and is a guide to help people empower their loved ones to "reality-test" and reclaim control of their minds and lives.

In 2014, I purchased the rights back to *Combating Cult Mind Control* and completed a substantial update. My friend and colleague Jon Atack, ex-Scientologist and cult expert, edited this new book with my request to add much missing material from the first edition on Scientology. Then, I launched a course on understanding cults a few years ago. You can find the link to that <u>here.</u>

This workbook was designed for the intensive <u>CE APA-approved course</u> for mental health professionals. With millions of people globally affected by radicalization or mind control and seeking professional assistance, clinicians must understand undue influence, cultism, dissociative disorders, and how to treat current or former cult members effectively. I am so happy you have decided to do this course because it means you are committed to aiding individuals in freeing themselves from undue influence, restoring their autonomy, and achieving freedom of mind. You can sign up for my Substack newsletter to receive weekly updates, where I share my insights and highlight the latest work from the Freedom of Mind team.

With the onslaught of Artificial Intelligence (AI) programs, including ChatGPT, Gemini, Copilot and others, Freedom of Mind © has registered itself as a trademark and has a trademark for The BITE Model of Authoritarian Control ™, a copyright for The BITE Model.© and The Influence Continuum ©.

Please email us for permission to use the above in any publication and for research. Permission will almost certainly be granted for all scholarly work.

If you find any mistakes, please let us know by emailing center@freedomofmind.com. We also appreciate notifications about any difficulties accessing the sources. Thank you.

Sincerely,

Dr. Steven Hassan

HOW TO USE THIS WORKBOOK

I would like to provide some recommendations on how to optimize using this workbook with your busy life and schedule.

It is advisable to determine your degree of commitment to this process before beginning. Considering your other obligations and responsibilities, use your calendar to schedule time you hope to devote to learning.

We have made the course primarily into 9 segments so you can do smaller bits in one sitting. Ensure your plan is feasible, and remember to include time for rest and integration. The workbook will be a way to digest what you are learning with the course and integrate it into your personal and professional life.

Proceed at a comfortable pace, as some of the content requires adequate time for integration. I have also included a list of the resources mentioned in each video lesson, found at the end of each corresponding module in the workbook. Each part of the workbook requires you to integrate what you have learned in the module. This design will deepen your learning of the content and help you make personal connections.

If you are a former cult member or have a loved one in a cult, I recommend that you have support systems in place, such as strategies for taking a break and people with whom you can talk to process ideas. Be self-aware. If you feel overwhelmed and unable to continue, you should take a break and return to the course when you feel prepared. As a side note, we intend to create a community of clinicians with future online classes to help fine-tune and support students in this class.

You can repeat this course as often as necessary, so there is no need to rush or try to process everything in one go, risking feeling overwhelmed. Perhaps you might wish to take the course as a whole first and then go back through it a second time, completing the workbook as you go.

I hope this course equips you with the knowledge and tools needed to understand cult mind control and aid individuals in their journey toward healing.

Scan the QR code or visit website (www.freedomofmind.com/workbook) to access resources that come with this workbook.

MODULE 1: UNDERSTANDING CULT MIND CONTROL

Summary: Introduces the concept of cult mind control through the biopsycho-social framework, highlighting the various types of cults, the BITE Model, and symptoms of undue influence.

Learning Objectives: Equip therapists with a foundational knowledge of cult operations and influence, enabling them to identify signs of undue influence and support affected clients.

In today's Information Age, now more than ever our minds are assaulted with a constant barrage of messaging that seeks to influence us, radicalize us, and bring us under the influence of external figureheads or creators. Anyone can start a blog, record a short video, and spread their ideas to impressionable individuals online. Influencers hold amazing sway over their captive audiences eagerly awaiting each new post or update. Political cults are becoming a mainstream part of our culture and the divide widens each day. At the same time, longstanding issues of offline cults, domestic violence, and elder abuse have not diminished or disappeared. Many professionals in the mental health field have no knowledge or experience in helping individuals leave these influences so that they can begin to regain their agency and live their lives to their fullest, truest potential again. Picking up this book is the first step in understanding why individuals fall prey to these cult influences and how to help them think for themselves once again.

To effectively work with individuals in cults, therapists are well advised to invest time researching the specific cult and gaining a deeper understanding of its nature. This process may involve taking additional classes or courses and speaking with former cult members. It might mean getting supervised. I plan to develop an online community for clinicians to be able to have access to my vast database of resources and people. This course aims to provide crucial information about cults, mind control, and cult recovery to better equip therapists in helping their clients.

UTILIZE A BIOPSYCHOSOCIAL FRAMEWORK

In the health field, we now understand that our wellness is framed by a multitude of factors, both internal and external. We call these compounding factors *biopsychosocial*—they consist of our genetic predispositions determined by biology, our intrinsic psychology which includes our personal feelings or reactions to stressors, and social factors which have been impressed upon us by our family, peers, and cultural expectations since birth.

Being primarily concerned with cults, a social phenomenon, a lot of my focus over the last five decades of my career has been on social psychology. As our understanding of human nature and psychology grow and deepen, we can also begin to understand and incorporate biological reasons why someone may join a cult—like brain chemicals or genetic predispositions that may cause someone to seek out strong group connections or spiritual guidance—as well as psychological factors that make someone susceptible to cult influence. Understanding susceptibilities to this type of influence and groupthink is essential for combatting these influences and helping individuals regain their free will.

TYPES OF CULTS

Over the past decade, the destructive cult phenomenon has escalated into a problem of enormous social and political importance. If therapists ignore the possibility of authoritarian and systemic social influence, they may not be treating the root cause of the patient's symptoms. That is why learning about the many types of cults is essential.

When people hear the word "cult" they typically think of religious cults. Still, authoritarian mind control is not limited to isolated religious sects. It is widespread across many segments of society:

- *Conspiracy cults* — e.g., 9/11 Truthers, FlatEarthers,
- *Psyops ('psychological operations)* — Fourth Generation Warfare (Fourth Generation Warfare involves decentralized, non-state actors using asymmetric tactics in blurred military and civilian arenas), QAnon
- *Online radicalization* — e.g., ISIS online recruitment, lone-actor terrorism too
- *Religious or spiritual cults* — e.g., the Moon cult, Falun Gong, New Apostolic Reformation, I AM, Channeling, Psychedelic cults
- *Multi-level marketing cults* — pyramid schemes including crypto and other MLMs
- *Political cults* — e.g., Russia, China, MAGA, North Korea, LaRouche Political Action Committee (linked to Lyndon LaRouche, exhibits cult-like devotion to

unorthodox economic and political ideas, led by a charismatic figure)

- *One-on-one cults* — domestic abuse, coercive control
- *Pseudo-therapy/educational cults* — include some coaching and self-help groups.

As a therapist, failing to recognize mind control in a client may result in missing crucial information needed to help them. We live in an age of influence in which mind control takes many forms. Hence, therapists must understand what is happening worldwide and how unhealthy influence affects people.

MIND CONTROL AND THE DSM-V-TR

The DSM-V-TR recognizes the effect of mind control. However, many clinicians are unaware that the DSM-V-TR, as well as the IV and III, have a category that recognizes the psychological impact of mind control. It used to be Unspecified Dissociative Disorder 300.15 (2013). It is now called Other Specified Dissociative Disorder (F44.89):

This category applies to presentations in which symptoms characteristic of a dissociative disorder that cause clinically significant distress or impairment in social, occupational, or other important areas of functioning predominate but do not meet the full criteria for any of the disorders in the dissociative disorders diagnostic class. The other specified dissociative disorder category is used in situations in which the clinician chooses to communicate the specific reason that the presentation does not meet the criteria for any specific dissociative disorder. This is done by recording "other specified dissociative disorder" followed by the specific reason (e.g., "dissociative trance")

2. Identity disturbance due to prolonged and intense coercive persuasion:

Individuals who have been subjected to intense coercive persuasion (e.g., brainwashing, thought reform, indoctrination while captive, torture, long-term political imprisonment, recruitment by sects/cults or by terror organizations) may present with prolonged changes in, or conscious questioning of, their identity."

REFLECTIVE EXERCISES

1. What comes to mind when you hear the word "cult?" Draw an image, list some words, or write a definition.

_____

_____

_____

_____

_____

_____
_____
_____
_____
_____
_____
_____
_____
_____
_____
_____
_____
_____
_____

CASE STUDY — LAURA

Module 1 of the course presents a video made during a two-hour program for one of the foremost experts in trauma, Dr. Judith Herman, author of *Trauma and Recovery*. The video is of a former client and a former cult member, Laura. Below is Laura's story:

Laura was raised a Christian, and her father was a minister. She describes having a reasonably normal childhood until she was 12, when her parents divorced, and her home life was disrupted. She was recruited into the International Churches of Christ cult at age 18 and remained there for nearly 13 years. During this time, she was also in an abusive marriage — she had been paired up with her husband and told she had to submit herself to him.

Laura left the cult in 2002. In the years following her exit, Laura engaged in self-injurious behavior and had multiple suicide attempts. She struggled with the mental health system for 11 years. She was misdiagnosed with borderline personality disorder, prescribed many medications, and received treatment — Dialectical Behavioral Therapy — which was inappropriate for her needs. Over time, her functional level improved dramatically, but she was still plagued with self-harm urges and dissociation so severe that she felt like an entity was inside her apartment.

In 2012, Laura finally received intensive cult-related counseling with me — approximately 30 hours over one week. She was given psychoeducation and taught about cult mind control and how to develop an internal locus of control. Laura is currently off all medication and no longer struggles with self-harm urges. She is a nurse and went on to get a PhD. She is married, has two children, and is doing great.

REFLECTIVE EXERCISES

Note: Complete the following reflective exercises after watching the video with Laura in Module 1.

2. What were Laura's situational vulnerabilities that contributed to her being more susceptible to being recruited into a cult? List them below.

_____

_____

_____

_____

_____

_____

_____

_____

_____

_____

_____

_____

3. The professionals working with Laura failed to recognize the specific impact of cult involvement on her mental health. By misdiagnosing her with borderline personality disorder and prescribing medications unsuited to her situation, they overlooked the necessity of addressing the root cause of her distress — her cult experiences and exit trauma.

_____

_____

_____

4. What could they have done differently?

HEALTHY AND UNHEALTHY SOCIAL INFLUENCE

Teaching individuals about discerning ethical from unethical influence is crucial to helping former or current cult members to begin evaluating their experiences. Many cult members have a binary, all-or-nothing thinking pattern, so it is essential to introduce them to the notion that reality is much more complex, nuanced, and sophisticated.

Social influence operates on a continuum from healthy to unhealthy, with groups exerting influence at different points along this spectrum. I call this model The Influence Continuum. Healthy influence is based on truth, honesty, genuine care, love, friendship, and community. On the other hand, unhealthy, destructive influence exhibits attributes of authoritarianism. It is characterized by deception, lying, distorting or withholding information, and affection being made conditional upon obedience to the rules. Please see the next page for an image of the Influence Continuum.

THE INFLUENCE CONTINUUM — INDIVIDUALS

The Influence Continuum assumes people should enjoy freedom of choice, critical thinking, compassion, conscience, creativity, humor, and unconditional love. An individual should also be free to express their authentic self. Being born into a cult presents unique challenges in this area. A cult upbringing can confuse one's identity and self, making therapy a valuable tool in helping clients discover their unique personality and build a positive self-concept.

The biopsychosocial framework recognizes that every person's genetic code, psychological adaptation, and environment are unique. However, under unhealthy influence, a false identity, or "pseudo-self" emerges, modeled after the cult leader or what the cult considers the appropriate way of being.

At the harmful end of the continuum, "love" is conditional. The cult may claim to treat its members as part of a "family" and promise love and care. Still, this so-called "love" is only given in exchange for obedience and conformity. This kind of "love" contrasts with unconditional love, even when a person's beliefs or behaviors may not align with yours.

In healthy groups, individuals trust their instincts and inner voice, but in authoritarian cults, the cult's doctrine is portrayed as the ultimate "truth," causing individuals to ignore or suppress their emotions and experiences.

Creative expression and healthy humor are prevalent in ethical groups. Subversive humor is often rare when you are a member of an authoritarian cult — you cannot make fun of the leader, doctrine, or policies.

Further, guilt, manipulation, fear, and indoctrination is used to control cult members. There is little room for creativity or fun.

FREEDOM OF MIND®
RESOURCE CENTER

INFLUENCE CONTINUUM©

TO BE USED WITH THE BITE MODEL OF AUTHORITARIAN CONTROL™
BEHAVIOR, INFORMATION, THOUGHT & EMOTIONAL CONTROL

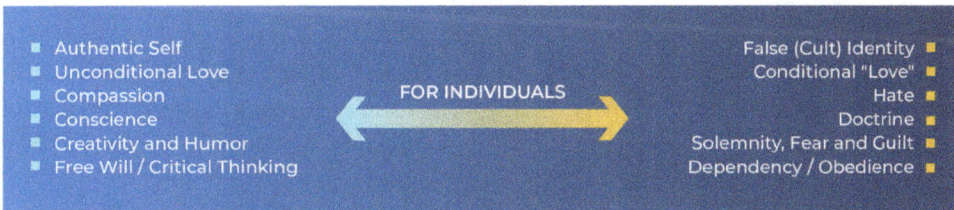

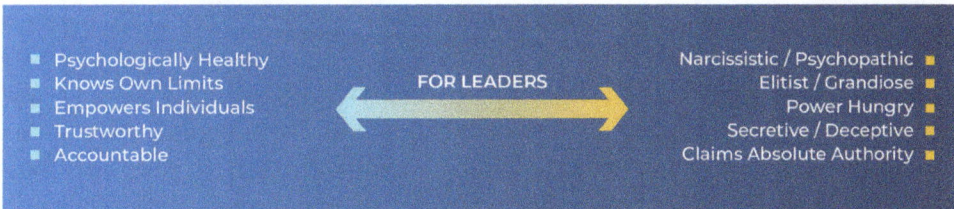

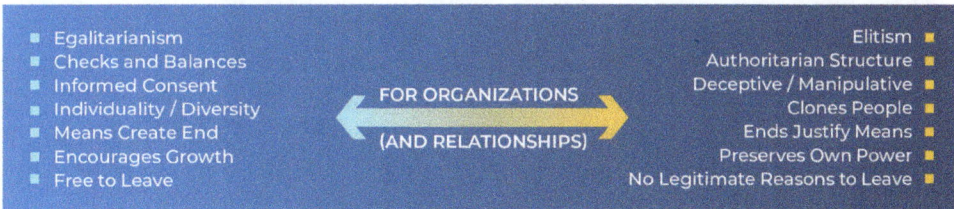

CONSTRUCTIVE	← →	DESTRUCTIVE
HEALTHY		UNHEALTHY

FOR INDIVIDUALS

Authentic Self	False (Cult) Identity
Unconditional Love	Conditional "Love"
Compassion	Hate
Conscience	Doctrine
Creativity and Humor	Solemnity, Fear and Guilt
Free Will / Critical Thinking	Dependency / Obedience

FOR LEADERS

Psychologically Healthy	Narcissistic / Psychopathic
Knows Own Limits	Elitist / Grandiose
Empowers Individuals	Power Hungry
Trustworthy	Secretive / Deceptive
Accountable	Claims Absolute Authority

FOR ORGANIZATIONS (AND RELATIONSHIPS)

Egalitarianism	Elitism
Checks and Balances	Authoritarian Structure
Informed Consent	Deceptive / Manipulative
Individuality / Diversity	Clones People
Means Create End	Ends Justify Means
Encourages Growth	Preserves Own Power
Free to Leave	No Legitimate Reasons to Leave

Freedom of Mind Resource Center, Inc.

FROM COMBATING CULT MIND CONTROL (2018) BY STEVEN HASSAN

freedomofmind.com

In a healthy group, members have the autonomy to think about the information they are presented with to "reality test." (Reality testing is a process that involves checking your thoughts and perceptions to see if they align with the real world. It is a way to differentiate between what is real and what might be influenced by internal biases, emotions, or misinformation. In an authoritarian cult, individuals are dependent and obedient.

THE INFLUENCE CONTINUUM — LEADERS

Healthy leaders prioritize growth, learning, trustworthiness, accountability, and empowering those they lead or work with. They take responsibility for their mistakes and are aware of their limitations. They delegate roles and tasks to others.

Unethical leaders are usually malignant narcissists, which means they exhibit the following characteristics: grandiose self-centered behavior, fantasies of power, success, and attractiveness, need for praise and admiration, sense of entitlement, lack of empathy, antisocial behavior, lying, interpersonally exploitative, sadism, harassment and silencing, violence, paranoia. Find out more at my webpage devoted to explaining malignant narcissism.

In general, a desire for power drives malignant narcissists and they are secretive and deceptive, claiming absolute authority. Some religious cult leaders claim to be divinely ordained as prophets or apostles. Some cult leaders actually claim to be God. They speak with certainty and believe themselves to be above others.

THE INFLUENCE CONTINUUM — ORGANIZATIONS

Healthy groups have checks and balances and promote diversity, equality, and non-discrimination. They offer ongoing informed consent, encourage personal growth, and allow individuals to leave if they are unhappy. Healthy organizations wish their members well whether or not they are regularly engaging with the organization and maintain open communication.

On the other hand, authoritarian cults exhibit elitism, adopt a hierarchical structure, and manipulate their members. They force conformity to the leader's image and prioritize the preservation of the group above all else, even at the cost of perpetuating harmful practices such as abuse. Leaving the group is discouraged and portrayed as a personal flaw, with the leader, doctrine, and policies upheld as the only truth.

Healthy organizations foster open communication, informed consent, and personal growth, while authoritarian groups enforce conformity and control to maintain their power and influence.

REFLECTIVE EXERCISES

5. Reflect on a healthy group you have been in and what this experience was like. What were some of the elements that made it healthy?

_____

_____

_____

_____

_____

_____

_____

_____

_____

_____

_____

_____

_____

THE BITE MODEL

To evaluate where a group falls on the Influence Continuum, I have proposed a four-part, overlapping model of looking at behavior, information, thought, and emotional control. The more a group seeks to control any or all of these aspects of its members' lives, the closer it falls to the unhealthy end of the Influence Continuum — and the more likely it is to be an authoritarian cult. The following pages contain information about the BITE Model.

Many erroneously believe mind control is an ambiguous, mystical process that cannot be defined in concrete terms. However, mind control involves specific methods and techniques influencing a person's thoughts, feelings, and acts. By consulting the Influence Continuum and using the BITE Model, we can analyze whether or not a leader or group is seeking to exert undue influence to control their followers.

SYMPTOMS OF UNDUE INFLUENCE

When a therapist addresses clinical concerns with a client who is a current or former cult member, the client may describe various issues. These problems can result from various causes and do not necessarily indicate mind control.

However, suppose the client has been part of a group known for abusive behavior and mind control. In that case, the therapist can expect to see some of the following symptoms:

1. *Extreme identity confusion* — particularly for individuals born into cults who believe their only identity is the cult identity. The therapist should begin uncovering their client's authentic self and demonstrating to the person that they have personal interests and orientations. Therapists can help clients identify instances in their lives when they rebelled, had doubts, or desired to do something other than what they were told. These moments are indicative of the person's authentic self.

2. *Dissociative states* — "floating" is when a former cult member mentally reverts to their group involvement and starts thinking from within their cult identity.

3. *Panic and anxiety attacks* — often a result of phobia indoctrination where irrational fears are instilled about leaving the group or challenging the leader's authority. These phobias maintain followers' dependence and obedience. While medication may be necessary in severe cases, clients can be empowered to cope with their stress and anxiety through techniques such as meditation and relaxation.

4. *Depression* — leaving a cult can lead to confusion, shame, loneliness, and depression as individuals come to terms with being lied to and manipulated. Therapists need to support former members in acknowledging and processing their pain. Engaging in activities such as daily walks in nature and aerobic exercise can be beneficial in elevating mood without relying on medication.

5. *Post-traumatic stress disorder* (PTSD) - the experience of being manipulated, controlled, and subjected to psychological abuse can be traumatic and lead to symptoms of PTSD.

6. *Psychosomatic symptoms* (such as headaches, backaches, and asthma) — according to the embodied mind approach, our bodies are the external manifestation of

Dr. Steven Hassan's
BITE MODEL
of Authoritarian Control™

FREEDOM
OF MIND®
RESOURCE CENTER

BEHAVIOR CONTROL

1. Regulate individual's physical reality
2. Dictate where, how, and with whom the member lives and associates or isolates
3. When, how and with whom the member has sex
4. Control types of clothing and hairstyles
5. Regulate diet - food and drink, hunger and/or fasting
6. Manipulation and deprivation of sleep
7. Financial exploitation, manipulation or dependence
8. Restrict leisure, entertainment, vacation time
9. Major time spent with group indoctrination and rituals and/or self indoctrination including the Internet
10. Permission required for major decisions
11. Rewards and punishments used to modify behaviors, both positive and negative
12. Discourage individualism, encourage group-think
13. Impose rigid rules and regulations
14. Punish disobedience by beating, torture, burning, cutting, rape, or tattooing/branding
15. Threaten harm to family and friends
16. Force individual to rape or be raped
17. Encourage and engage in corporal punishment
18. Instill dependency and obedience
19. Kidnapping
20. Beating
21. Torture
22. Rape
23. Separation of Families
24. Imprisonment
25. Murder

INFORMATION CONTROL

1. Deception:
a. Deliberately withhold information
b. Distort information to make it more acceptable
c. Systematically lie to the cult member

2. Minimize or discourage access to non-cult sources of information, including:
a. Internet, TV, radio, books, articles, newspapers, magazines, media
b. Critical information
c. Former members
d. Keep members busy so they don't have time to think and investigate
e. Control through cell phone with texting, calls, internet tracking

3. Compartmentalize information into Outsider vs. Insider doctrines
a. Ensure that information is not freely accessible
b. Control information at different levels and missions within group
c. Allow only leadership to decide who needs to know what and when

4. Encourage spying on other members
a. Impose a buddy system to monitor and control member
b. Report deviant thoughts, feelings and actions to leadership
c. Ensure that individual behavior is monitored by group

5. Extensive use of cult-generated information and propaganda, including:
a. Newsletters, magazines, journals, audiotapes, videotapes, YouTube, movies and other media
b. Misquoting statements or using them out of context from non-cult sources

6. Unethical use of confession
a. Information about sins used to disrupt and/or dissolve identity boundaries
b. Withholding forgiveness or absolution
c. Manipulation of memory, possible false memories

Dr. Steven Hassan's
BITE MODEL
of Authoritarian Control™

FREEDOM
OF MIND®
RESOURCE CENTER

THOUGHT CONTROL

1. Require members to internalize the group's doctrine as truth
a. Adopting the group's 'map of reality' as reality
b. Instill black and white thinking
c. Decide between good vs. evil
d. Organize people into us vs. them (insiders vs. outsiders)

2. Change person's name and identity

3. Use of loaded language and cliches which constrict knowledge, stop critical thoughts and reduce complexities into platitudinous buzz words

4. Encourage only 'good and proper' thoughts

5. Hypnotic techniques are used to alter mental states, undermine critical thinking and even to age regress the member

6. Memories are manipulated and false memories are created

7. Teaching thought-stopping techniques which shut down reality testing by stopping negative thoughts and allowing only positive thoughts, including:
a. Denial, rationalization, justification, wishful thinking
b. Chanting
c. Meditating
d. Praying
e. Speaking in tongues f. Singing or humming

8. Rejection of rational analysis, critical thinking, constructive criticism

9. Forbid critical questions about leader, doctrine, or policy allowed

10. Labeling alternative belief systems as illegitimate, evil, or not useful

11. Instill new "map of reality"

EMOTIONAL CONTROL

1. Manipulate and narrow the range of feelings – some emotions and/or needs are deemed as evil, wrong or selfish

2. Teach emotion-stopping techniques to block feelings of homesickness, anger, doubt

3. Make the person feel that problems are always their own fault, never the leader's or the group's fault

4. Promote feelings of guilt or unworthiness, such as
a. Identity guilt
b. You are not living up to your potential
c. Your family is deficient
d. Your past is suspect
e. Your affiliations are unwise
f. Your thoughts, feelings, actions are irrelevant or selfish
g. Social guilt
h. Historical guilt

5. Instill fear, such as fear of:
a. Thinking independently
b. The outside world
c. Enemies
d. Losing one's salvation
e. Leaving or being shunned by the group
f. Other's disapproval

6. Extremes of emotional highs and lows – love bombing and praise one moment and then declaring you are horrible sinner

7. Ritualistic and sometimes public confession of sins

8. Phobia indoctrination: inculcating irrational fears about leaving the group or questioning the leader's authority
a. No happiness or fulfillment possible outside of the group
b. Terrible consequences if you leave: hell, demon possession, incurable diseases, accidents, suicide, insanity, 10,000 reincarnations, etc.
c. Shunning of those who leave; fear of being rejected by friends and family
d. Never a legitimate reason to leave; those who leave are weak, undisciplined, unspiritual, worldly, brainwashed by family or counselor, or seduced by money, sex, or rock and roll
e. Threats of harm to ex-member and family

7. our minds. Hence, physical symptoms such as headaches, backaches, and asthma can sometimes indicate underlying psychological issues.

8. *Decision-making dependency* — unethical mind control impairs an individual's mature, autonomous decision-making ability. Therapists can help clients by offering psychoeducation and teaching decision-making strategies.

9. *Guilt* — former cult members may experience feelings of guilt for actions they took while in the group, such as recruiting others or manipulating them to leave their families or careers. Therapists must help clients understand that they are under the influence of mind control and not acting of their own free will.

10. *Fear* — former cult members may experience irrational fears instilled by the cult's programming and realistic fears of retaliation from those still within the group.

11. *Sleep disorders/nightmares* — members often experience sleep deprivation in cults while in the group. Therapists can help clients by discussing the importance of healthy sleep habits. Recurrent nightmares can signal unresolved emotional conflicts and indicate a need for further therapeutic support to process the impact of the cult experience.

12. *Eating disorders* — dietary changes frequently occur during cult involvement. Some groups encourage fasting with little consideration for physical well-being. There is sometimes drastic weight loss or gain. When and how people eat and their attitude toward food impacts their sense of self.

13. *Sexuality issues* — many authoritarian cults control relationships, including their member's sex lives. Some groups require members to deny or suppress sexual feelings, while others engage in sexual promiscuity, exploitation, or abuse.

14. *Money issues* — involvement in a cult may result in a changed relationship with money and a hindered approach to healthy financial practices, as members are often expected to donate significant amounts of their funds and assets to the group or to participate in fundraising.

15. *Lack of trust, fear of intimacy and commitment* — former cult members often feel so betrayed and abused that they have difficulty trusting any other group or authority figure and may fear entering into committed relationships. Clients can be helped to reclaim personal power and trust through psychoeducation and practice exercising their own decision-making. The Influence Continuum and BITE Model can allow people to do a reality test and know whether a group or relationship is trustworthy.

16. *Delayed or halted psychological development, loss of psychological power* — cult members are often subjected to high control and manipulation, which restricts

their personal growth and autonomy. They may become dependent on the cult leader for their sense of identity and purpose.

17. *Harassment and threats* — former cult members can face harassment, threats, lawsuits, blackmail, and even physical harm, mainly if an ex-member goes public. Since cults believe that anyone who leaves is an enemy, there is always some risk that harm might be done to a defector. There may be a need to involve law enforcement or for a client to enter a witness protection program if there is any safety risk.

18. *Grief* — leaving a cult after long-term involvement can lead to feelings of loss for missed opportunities in life, such as lacking a spouse or partner, children, education, career, and friends. Therapists can help clients process their grief and loss and view it as a chance for healing.

19. *Spiritual abuse, 'rape of the soul'* — former cult members may experience a profound sense of violation as they realize that the person they had given their love, trust, and commitment to was false and used them.

IS YOUR CLIENT UNDER MIND CONTROL?

The only way to determine if a client has been subjected to mind control is through asking questions and observing their reactions and responses. For example, a change in the client's facial expression may indicate a switch to their cult identity, but it is not always obvious.

Understanding whether your client has been under mind control is crucial for the therapeutic process. Misdiagnosis can prolong or hinder treatment and cause additional psychological trauma, so understanding the process and the effects of mind control can help protect clients from further harm.

It is also essential to avoid making assumptions that a client's symptoms are solely a result of mind control just because they are involved in a group. Some individuals may be highly engaged in a community that falls on the more harmless end of the Influence Continuum.

Mind control often creates phobias, delusions, paranoia, anxiety/panic attacks, dissociation, and a dual identity (false self vs. authentic self). To determine if these symptoms are related to mind control, it is necessary to explore the individual's experiences. For example, when did they first develop a phobia? Did they hear about it from someone else? Were they told something in a religious setting? These questions can help determine the origin of the symptoms.

ASSESSMENT

It is crucial to conduct a thorough assessment. Considering past and current circumstances is crucial. I always recommend beginning with assessing the present. For example:

- Are they eating and sleeping well and in a safe environment?

- Are they still in contact with the cult?

- Are they in touch with former members who have processed their experience and healed from it?

- Are they still doing any cult rituals? These can be internal, such as speaking in tongues, chanting, meditating, and uttering affirmations.

- Do they have family or friends that are still in the cult?

- Are they geographically distanced from cult buildings and members?

Once you have established their circumstances in the present, you can examine the past. If a client was born into the cult, this approach will require more focus and skill building.

CLIENTS MAY NOT REALIZE THEY ARE UNDER MIND CONTROL

Individuals under undue influence typically have a distorted perception of their situation:

- They believe it is their own free choice. They may still wrongly believe they chose to join. An illusion of choice makes them feel like they did this to themselves. The fact is that they were deceptively recruited and socially influenced into the cult.

- Some groups program members to believe there is no such thing as a victim. They are told they created their "reality" and did this to themselves.

- Their ability to think independently is suppressed through being programmed to always look outside themselves to a "leader" to tell them what to do.

- They live in a cult-induced bubble and are isolated from alternative perspectives and critical information.

- They have been limited in their ability to take other perspectives, especially in their own life.

Helping people understand social psychology and realize they are victims of undue influence is a big step in helping them to liberate themselves.

REFLECTIVE EXERCISE

6. In your experience, what are the top five symptoms of undue influence you have observed in other people who have been in cults (whether you have interacted with them personally or not)?

_____

_____

_____

_____

_____

_____

_____

_____

_____

_____

_____

_____

SET YOUR GOALS

7. If you are a mental health professional working with clients who have experienced cult mind control, it is important to set short- and long-term goals to acquire the necessary skills and knowledge to help these clients.

Identify a minimum of three things you can do *outside* this course to develop your skills and knowledge about cults:

1._____

_____

_____

2._____

_____

_____

3._____

_____

_____

CONCLUSION

Therapists are essential in supporting individuals subjected to cults or other forms of mind control. To provide adequate support, therapists must possess an in-depth understanding of the dynamics of undue influence. Clients may not recognize that they have been under mind control and may hold distorted views of their situation. By guiding clients to comprehend their experiences, therapists can empower former cult members to understand they have been subjected to mind control and aid them in their journey of liberation.

MODULE 1 RESOURCES

Books

Influence by Robert Cialdini

Explores persuasion psychology, introducing six principles: Reciprocity, Commitment, Social Proof, Authority, Liking, and Scarcity. Essential for understanding and applying persuasive techniques.

Trauma and Recovery by Dr. Judith Herman

A comprehensive examination of psychological trauma and recovery stages. Offers insights into trauma's effects and healing paths, emphasizing the importance of understanding trauma's impact.

Lone-Actor Terrorism, Chapter by Dr. Steven Hassan

This Oxford University Press textbook analyzes the psychology behind lone-actor terrorism, including motivations and social-psychological factors. It is essential for understanding the individual paths to radicalization and violence.

Waking the Tiger: Healing Trauma by Peter Levine

Introduces somatic experiencing for trauma treatment, emphasizing the body's healing capabilities. Offers innovative approaches to releasing traumatic stress and restoring balance.

The Brain That Changes Itself by Norman Doidge

It presents neuroplasticity, showing how the brain can rewire after injury or trauma. Offers hope through stories of recovery and transformation.

A History of God by Karen Armstrong

Traces the evolution of the concept of God in Judaism, Christianity, and Islam. Offers a comprehensive overview of how the idea of God has changed over millennia.

Feeling Good by David Burns MD

Introduces cognitive behavioral therapy techniques for overcoming depression. Emphasizes practical strategies for altering negative thought patterns and improving mood and self-esteem.

Websites

MLMconference

AAWA

Freedom of Mind Resources

QAnon and the BITE Model

Lorna and Bill Goldberg: Fifty Years of Helping People Out of Cults
How to Tell if You're Brainwashed — Dr. Steve Hassan's TEDx Boston

The BITE Model of Authoritarian Control — Dr. Steve Hassan's dissertation

MODULE 2: VULNERABILITY AND RECRUITMENT

Summary: Explores vulnerabilities that lead individuals to cult involvement and examines cult recruitment tactics.

Objectives: Teach therapists to recognize and understand vulnerabilities and recruitment methods, aiding clients in overcoming cult influence.

Many mistakenly believe that only weak, "stupid", or uneducated people get involved in destructive cults. This denial of reality allows individuals to distance themselves from the possibility that they, too, could fall victim to cult recruitment. Law professor emeritus Alan Scheflin calls this "the myth of the unmalleable mind."

The most important thing to realize in dealing with destructive cults is that we are human beings, and, therefore, we all have vulnerabilities. Most wish to improve themselves and their loved ones. We all crave happiness and affection and aspire for something greater in life, such as improved relationships, better health, wealth, wisdom, and status. Unfortunately, these fundamental human needs and qualities are precisely what cult recruiters exploit.

We all need to accept that we can be deceived or tricked. Similarly, we must trust people and institutions with agendas in order to participate in society. The most we can do to protect ourselves from malicious influence is to inform ourselves about how predators and authoritarian cults operate and learn to be good consumers. Whenever we are asked to commit time, money, or our good name, we must independently research first. We should ask direct questions and demand direct and truthful answers. We should do research that seeks out facts and verifiable evidence. Informed consent is a process, so we must periodically reassess ongoing situations and seek new information. A trustworthy person or group must be able to stand up to scrutiny. The burden is on them to prove they are authentic, honest, and trustworthy.

Cult recruiters exploit fundamental human desires—such as self-improvement, desire to help others, belonging, and purpose—targeting anyone's vulnerabilities, regardless of their education or strength of mind.

THE FUNDAMENTAL ATTRIBUTION ERROR

One of the most important cognitive biases in social psychology is the fundamental attribution error. This is our tendency to assume that a person's actions reflect who they are or what they value rather than considering the situation they might be in or who they are with. If someone cuts you while you're driving in crowded traffic, do you consider that he or she might be in a rush due to an emergency or do you assume they are rude and reckless? This is a classical example of the fundamental attribution error. When humans wish to understand other people's actions, there is a universal bias to over attribute the behavior to internal or dispositional factors rather than social context or situational factors.

It is frightening to consider that someone could have control over us. When we hear about someone experiencing an adverse event, we often search for a cause, such as whether they were in the wrong place at the wrong time or what they may have done to contribute to their misfortune. When people commit the fundamental attribution error, they overestimate the role of the person's character, personality, or disposition and underestimate the power of the situation. "Blaming the victim" is a defensive psychological mechanism that creates a distance between the hurt person and us. It allows us to convince ourselves that such a situation could not happen to us because we are somehow different or know better.

When it comes to cult victims, the fundamental attribution error often causes them to blame the victim rather than understand the situation. They may assume that the person must be gullible, weak-minded, or have serious personality flaws that caused them to join an extreme control group. They attribute the victim's suffering to character weakness, overlooking the fact that cults use highly sophisticated, manipulative tactics to recruit and control people. Cult leaders are skilled at exploiting vulnerabilities, creating strong social pressure, and using psychological techniques to make members feel accepted, safe, and committed. By attributing the person's involvement to "flaws" rather than the cult's coercive influence, outsiders may lack empathy and perpetuate harmful stereotypes. This makes it even harder for former cult members to seek help, as they may feel stigmatized and misunderstood rather than supported in their recovery.

The fundamental attribution error makes it difficult for cult victims to leave the group or seek help. They may feel ashamed or embarrassed. They might fear being judged or blamed for their involvement in the cult. Recognizing the situational and environmental factors that contributed to their cult recruitment and the factors that kept them involved is a critically important step to exiting and some face-saving with family and friends. Being able to articulate the role of manipulation and coercion in these processes can help to counter the stigma that can surround cult victims.

The fundamental attribution error highlights the need to take a more holistic approach to understanding the behavior of others and not rely solely on personal variables. Therefore, mental health practitioners must understand how the fundamental attribution error applies to people's perceptions of cult victims and be able to explain it to clients.

REFLECTIVE EXERCISES

1. Select the most the five most typical words people might use to describe a cult victim:

☐ Weak	☐ Uninhibited	☐ Self-controlled	☐ Cautious	☐ Bold	☐ Trusting
☐ Skeptical	☐ Gullible	☐ Realistic	☐ Unassuming	☐ Idealistic	☐ Subjective
☐ Analytical	☐ Self-asserting	☐ Lighthearted	☐ Talkative	☐ Serious	☐ Quiet

2. How might each word you chose affect a former cult member's ability to share their experiences?

_____

_____

_____

_____

_____

_____

_____

_____

_____

_____

_____

_____

_____

_____

3. Which of the following examples show the fundamental attribution error (select all that apply):

- A woman is upset with her brother for joining Scientology and believes he was gullible to be sucked in.
- A man believes his son joined the Unification Church because the recruiters deceived and manipulated him.
- A therapist believes his client has been unable to stop engaging in sex work because her pimp uses powerful strategies to control her.
- A woman believes her sister is failing to leave her controlling partner because she is too weak to stand up to him.

4. In the below table, you will complete a multi-step process to understand your own experiences with attribution. Think of three instances in your life in which someone behaved negatively toward you, and you attributed the mistreatment to the individual's character. Describe the negative behavior against you and what you perceived as the personality/character flaw. Then, list two possible situational causes explaining the person's behavior.

Observed Behavior	Perceived Personality Flaw	1st Possible Situational Cause	2nd Possible Situational Cause
Example: A car sped past me and cut me off on my way to work	The driver is reckless and rude	The driver's wife was in labor, and he was rushing to the hospital	A wasp flew into the car, and the driver rushed to get to an area to pull over.

5. Reflect on a time when you were hurt or frustrated by someone's actions. Did you make assumptions about their character? What were they? With what you now know about the fundamental attribution error, list some other factors that may have caused their behavior. Does this change how you feel about the situation?

_____

_____

_____

_____

_____

_____

_____

_____

_____

_____

_____

_____

_____

VULNERABILITIES TO CULT RECRUITMENT

No one actively wishes to join a destructive cult, to be exploited, abused, taken advantage of, or enslaved. The reason why people find themselves in their manipulative, high-control groups is because recruiters use deception through lying, withholding, or distorting vital information to create the illusion of an appealing and welcoming community. Therefore, it is essential to acknowledge that people are not actively seeking to join destructive cults; instead, cults proactively seek out and recruit individuals.

Deceptive recruitment can lure anyone, particularly those experiencing situational vulnerability, like losing a loved one or ending a romantic relationship. Our world is becoming increasingly socially isolated. The COVID-19 pandemic caused prolonged social isolation and financial struggles, causing people who have been desperate for connection and prosperity to become increasingly vulnerable to online recruitment and indoctrination.

Of course, there are also many individual vulnerabilities, such as learning and developmental disabilities, addictions, or early childhood trauma. The most significant vulnerability that leaves individuals susceptible to cult recruitment, however, is a lack of education about techniques used for cult mind control and undue influence

SITUATIONAL VULNERABILITIES

Research involving current and former cult members has shown that a notable proportion of those who get into destructive cults were approached during vulnerable moments. For instance, if someone's parents divorce, they may be more susceptible to a recruiter who presents the group as a happy family or portrays the leader as an ideal parental figure, as was the case in my former cult.

Situational vulnerabilities — upheaval at home, the pain of a breakup or parental divorce, grief from losing a loved one — can make anyone susceptible to undue influence and cult recruitment. Major life transitions like a recent illness, job loss, graduation, or moving to a new place can also create a sense of instability, leaving people searching for support and direction. Societal factors like uncertainty due to political instability or a global pandemic create stress which affects our bodies and minds. This weakening of our natural defenses can allow red flags and warning signs to go unnoticed.

Moving frequently, for example, as with military families or certain employment circumstances, can cause some disruption and make people more open to making new "friends." Immigrant populations can be exceptionally vulnerable when they arrive in a new city, state, or country as they try to adapt to the culture and language, make connections, and be open to new ideas without knowing how to discern or ask the right questions.

INDIVIDUAL VULNERABILITIES

Many individual vulnerabilities can make someone more susceptible to cult recruitment. Some of these include:

1.	*Hypnotizability* — Hypnosis is not sleep. It is a heightened state of concentration that renders people more susceptible to suggestion. Highly hypnotizable individuals may be particularly susceptible to exploitation. High hypnotizable individuals have a "superpower," enabling them to accomplish remarkable feats, such as in sports, music, art, and writing. These people often have powerful imaginations.

One demonstration of this is a person could imagine holding a bag of ice on their palm, and they can make their skin temperature go down. It is a mistake to think only about TV-style "stage hypnotists" when understanding hypnosis. Clinical hypnotherapists can help people rewire their brains to install healthy new beliefs, control pain, sleep more deeply, and improve memory and concentration.

Aside from being born with this gift, people can be taught to go into deep trance states. However, participation in a group that exploits hypnotic training routines — like Scientology — can make people dissociated and, therefore, less able to think critically.

"Guided meditations" are often hypnotic suggestions that can bypass conscious awareness. These resemble hypnosis and can increase vulnerability. This phenomenon also occurs online, where individuals may become immersed in "doomscrolling" or spend hours clicking on suggested AI-generated links. This intense fixation can be a vulnerability if the individual cannot make informed decisions beforehand or regulate their behavior.

2.   *Learning and Developmental Disorders* - People with learning and developmental disorders, like ADHD, dyslexia, or other cognitive challenges, often carry a lifetime of feeling "different," misunderstood, or less capable than their peers. These experiences can lead to low self-esteem, heightened sensitivity to rejection, and a need for affirmation — making them more vulnerable to manipulation and recruitment into cults or high-control groups. Without adequate support, they may develop coping mechanisms that leave them open to influence by others who offer validation, a sense of belonging, and "solutions" to their struggles. Cults are skilled at recognizing these vulnerabilities and may create messaging tailored to reach these individuals, framing the group as a place of acceptance or focused on self-improvement. Therapists must establish whether their clients have a learning disability and what steps they have taken to cope with it.

3.   *Autism Spectrum Disorder* - Individuals on the <u>autism spectrum</u> often bring incredible intelligence and insight to the table but may experience challenges in reading social cues, which can be used to manipulate and deceive them. Digital communication can feel safer and more manageable for individuals on the autism spectrum, who often struggle with social anxiety and specialized interests. However, this preference for online interaction can open doors to undue influence from predatory groups and cults. Online, it is much easier for high-control groups to obscure intentions and present a carefully curated image, leading to an environment where subtle manipulation is harder to detect. Without the physical context of face-to-face meetings—body language, tone shifts, or eye contact, individuals on the spectrum may find it even more challenging to pick up on the nonverbal cues that typically signal deceit, pressure, or coercion. High-control groups exploit this by grooming and recruiting online, creating a false sense of connection and community that can be hard to distinguish from genuine support.

For those particularly interested in this topic, refer to my <u>interview with world Asperger's authority Tony Attwood</u>.[1]

---

[1] Many of those with Autism Spectrum Disorder (ASD) who were previously diagnosed with Asperger's disorder prefer the latter term which is why I use it here.

4.   *Addictions* - Individuals struggling with drug, alcohol, internet, or other addictions may feel isolated, powerless, and disconnected from their communities. They may also have a sense of emptiness or a lack of meaning. As addiction takes hold, it can erode relationships with family, friends, and colleagues, leaving a person with a diminished social support system. This isolation feeds feelings of emptiness and a lack of meaning, which many high-control groups and cults skillfully exploit.

Furthermore, addiction affects critical thinking and judgment, reducing the individual's ability to recognize red flags or manipulative tactics. Recruiters know how to appeal to those looking to fill the void left by addiction, sometimes even portraying the group as a path to healing or self-improvement. In reality, the addictive cycle can shift from substance dependency to dependency on the group, with high-control leaders taking the place of the addictive behavior, offering emotional highs and lows that mimic addiction. It's essential for therapists and support networks to recognize these vulnerabilities in recovering addicts, empowering them with the tools to resist undue influence and build healthy, genuine connections outside of high-control environments.

5.   *Unresolved Sexual Issues* - Individuals who have experienced sexual abuse during childhood often carry deep wounds which profoundly impact their adult relationships. These individuals may unconsciously be drawn to charismatic figures or "gurus" who promise healing and emotional growth. The traumatic experiences from their past can create a complex need for validation and acceptance, leading them to seek out familiar dynamics in an attempt to gain closure or heal their wounds.

Unfortunately, many manipulative leaders have discovered ways to exploit this need for healing and growth, creating a carefully crafted image of wisdom and safety as "healers" or "mentors". This creates the illusion of a nurturing relationship, but over time, it often becomes exploitative. The individual might not recognize this manipulation, even when harmful patterns appear again. After all, the group or its leader have been presenting that they are the path to healing and growth. Therefore, it's imperative that survivors of abuse learn to identify these warning signs and understand how trauma impacts their relationship patterns in order to protect themselves from those who would take advantage of them.

6.   *Phobias* - People struggling with phobias often carry heightened fears and anxieties that can make them particularly susceptible to manipulation by cult recruiters. They may unconsciously reveal their specific fears — such as fear of illness, social anxieties, or even death — when speaking with a recruiter who has been trained to appear trustworthy and compassionate. These skilled manipulators take advantage of this vulnerability by framing the group's beliefs and practices

as a way to protect vulnerable individuals from these perceived threats.

Cult recruiters may offer assurances that the group will provide safety or divine protection against the individual's specific fears. For example, a person with anxieties regarding illnesses might be convinced that the group has unique insight into avoiding sickness and preserving health, while someone with social anxiety might be drawn to the promise of a supportive community. These tactics foster dependency on the group and amplify the belief that leaving would make them susceptible to the threats of the things they fear the most once again. It is vital for individuals with phobias to understand how their fears can be exploited by high control groups so they can make informed choices and maintain their autonomy.

REFLECTIVE EXERCISES

6. Identify three situational vulnerabilities in your own life that might make you more susceptible to undue influence.

_____

_____

_____

_____

_____

_____

_____

_____

_____

_____

7. List the key situational and/or individual vulnerabilities that may have contributed to the recruitment of a current or former cult member you have worked with in a therapeutic context. (You can also answer this question based on someone you know personally or have read about if you have not had clients who are cult members.)

Situational Vulnerabilities	Individual Vulnerabilities

In the digital age, cults use technology, social media, and AI to gather information about people to create profiles that can help bad actors perfect their recruitment and indoctrination strategies.

Living in the 21st century poses many challenges contributing to people's vulnerability to cult recruitment. Political polarization, psychological warfare, and conspiracy theories are being used to spread chaos and fear. The COVID-19 pandemic has also increased people's screen time, resulting in social isolation and making individuals more vulnerable to manipulation, particularly in countries without strong data privacy laws. Social media platforms are designed to capture people's attention. Many people are now online ten to fourteen hours a day, which can lead to an internet addiction.

The digital age has brought about a massive change in the way we think, feel, and communicate. Additionally, there is a digitalization of what cults are doing in real life, and groups like QAnon are simply replicating it online. The big difference is that, unlike physical recruitment, political and cult groups now have access to people's private information. Data about our preferences and choices has been harvested online to create sophisticated psychological profiles that can more easily target and influence people. We are entering a whole new level of manipulation and mind control.

Many technological factors may contribute to increased susceptibility to cult recruitment:

1. *The metaverse* — We are all being directed to expect to spend increasing amounts of time in a virtual universe where users can interact with a computer-generated environment. Facebook even changed its *name* to Meta. Apple now has its own virtual reality headset. These immersive experiences can potentially increase susceptibility to cult recruitment by blurring the lines between reality and fiction.

Although virtual reality (VR) can be used for beneficial purposes, such as therapy, exercise, reducing chronic pain by rewiring neural pathways, and providing an immersive experience for people with disabilities, any technology that can do good also has the potential to harm. Therefore, it's vital for individuals to be aware of the potential risks and to approach virtual environments with caution and critical thinking.

2. *Conscious and unconscious impact on the brain* - Avoiding screen exposure for children under three years old is common among tech-savvy individuals due to screens' effect on the brain, both consciously and unconsciously. According to Kahneman and Tversky's research, we have an unconscious mind that makes quick judgments based on predictive models (system 1) and a conscious mind that processes information rationally (system 2). By understanding the unconscious and identifying any biases it may hold, individuals can reduce their susceptibility to cult recruitment. It's possible to rewire the brain to adopt a healthier mindset.

3. *Personalized data collection* - The issue of personalized data collection was brought to the forefront with the Cambridge Analytica scandal, where they illegally obtained a vast amount of individuals' personal information through Facebook. Since then, there have been numerous instances of cyberhacking in which personal information, including social security numbers, phone numbers, and even the most minor details like eating habits and grocery purchases, are being harvested and can potentially be utilized for malicious purposes, including online cult recruitment. The United States has no data privacy laws due to extensive

lobbying and corruption of public officials. Europe is far ahead and proactively makes an effort to protect its people.

4.   *Artificial Intelligence* - Artificial Intelligence (AI) is a constantly evolving technology that can collect and analyze large amounts of data about individuals, including their behavior, preferences, and vulnerabilities. This information can be used to target individuals with personalized messages and persuasive content that is designed to exploit their emotions and vulnerabilities. ChatGPT4 uses large language models, but on the horizon is quantum computing, which will be far faster and able to perform much more sophisticated processing.

5.   *Psyops disinformation* - The term "psyops" refers to psychological operations that use a combination of false information and elements of truth to manipulate individuals' thoughts and beliefs. Psyops are a tactic used by military divisions and authoritarian groups to influence people's perception of reality. Russia calls these "active measures" and is using them extensively to manipulate public opinion and elections worldwide.

RECRUITMENT STRATEGIES

Authoritarian cults seek to recruit as many people as possible. Rarely is it a spontaneous occurrence. It is a systematic process that is used on people. The use of deception, hypnosis, and other forms of mind control to attract followers violates people's right to choose for themselves.

Usually, an individual does not realize they are being targeted for recruitment. A friend or family member may want to share fascinating new insights or experiences. They may even say they need your opinion and convince you to attend an indoctrination session. If the recruiter starts off a stranger, more often than not, by the end, you think you've made a good friend.

Various tactics employed by groups utilize mind control to lure people in. Several cults deliberately target intelligent, skilled, and accomplished individuals, making their members more compelling and convincing to newcomers. Cult members are conditioned to present only the favorable aspects of the organization, suppressing any negative emotions about the group and presenting a smiling, cheerful demeanor. The high number of devoted and sincere members that a recruit encounters is more convincing than any structure or doctrine that the group espouses.

IN-PERSON RECRUITMENT

Cult recruiters use various settings such as social events, work functions, churches, gyms, yoga studios, concerts, or rallies to establish personal contact with individuals.

First, the recruiters are instructed to gain insight into an individual's details, such as their hopes, fears, relationships, jobs, and interests. Then, they devise a strategic plan to induct the person into the group.

Love bombing can feel intoxicating, as overwhelming praise and attention make you feel seen, valued, and special. Online, love bombing is termed swarming by radicalization experts.

Many individuals I have worked with over the years have expressed being attracted to their recruiter and even falling in love with them. However, in most cases, the recruiter is not interested in a genuine relationship, but rather in getting their foot in the door and beginning the indoctrination process before eventually disappearing.

To illustrate how cult recruiters target individuals, I refer to the approach of the Moonies cult of strategically categorizing people for future manipulation. This was used to recruit me into the <u>Moon cult</u>, and I, in turn, used it to recruit others.

People were divided into four categories: Thinkers, Feelers, Doers, and Believers:

1.   *Thinkers* - If a person was categorized as a thinker, we would use an intellectual approach to recruitment. For example, we would show him pictures of Nobel Laureates at a Moonie-sponsored science conference or philosophers discussing various interesting topics.

2.   *Feelers* - For Feelers, the emphasis would be on "love bombing" and creating a sense of belonging and family. The recruiter would emphasize emotional well-being and the group's extended family aspect. Since feelers crave acceptance and affection, recruiters would make them feel warmly welcomed and approved unconditionally.

3.   *Doers* - Doers are focused on taking action, enjoying challenges, and achieving as much as possible. For example, if a doer expressed distress due to the poverty and suffering in the world, recruiters would convince them of the considerable work the group was doing to combat these issues.

4.   *Believers* - Believers are spiritually motivated, and therefore, the emphasis would be on religious or metaphysical discussions. Believers are usually very receptive and open to joining a religious or spiritual group and often recruit *themselves*. For example, I have encountered many cult members who had recently prayed to God to guide their lives, and so many thought they were divinely led to meet their recruiter.

Unfortunately, after many decades, the recruitment methods employed by cults have become more advanced and sophisticated, which increases their success in ensnaring new members.

ONLINE RECRUITMENT

Cults are not limited to in-person recruitment; they have embraced the digital world, too. The change in internet usage since the Covid-19 pandemic has laid the groundwork for more people to be recruited online than ever before. The internet has become a hunting ground for cults to find potential recruits, and they use various websites, social media platforms, online discussion groups, and messaging apps.

Cults may offer free online courses or resources designed to appeal to individuals searching for personal growth or spiritual development. They may also create online communities that provide a sense of belonging and connection to individuals who may be feeling isolated.

The dark web, known for illegal activities, also allows cults to gather personal information on individuals. In addition, video platforms like YouTube and Vimeo are also used to spread their message and influence. Many young people are recruited from online gaming sites.

Dating sites are also used for cult recruitment. In the past, even terrorist organizations like ISIS have used marriage and dating sites to lure people in. Recruiters may misrepresent themselves, using attractive profile pictures and engaging profile descriptions to make themselves seem like desirable matches. Once they connect with someone, they start engaging with them and trying to introduce them gradually to the cult. The technique of love bombing, in which multiple people shower praise on the individual, can be done online, too. The ultimate goal is to create a network that isolates the individual from their family and friends.

THE VICTIM BECOMES THE VICTIMIZER

The victim-victimizer model is when an individual is deceptively drawn into a group and then taught to recruit others using the same deceptive methods, perpetuating the harmful cycle.

Cults often use the buddy system, pairing recruits with more experienced members, who are often seen as spiritual leaders. For example, in some shepherding discipleship-based cults, recruits are encouraged to treat their "Shepherd" as if they were Jesus, confessing everything and being obedient to them completely. Recruits are then expected to recruit others and pass on the mind control techniques.

When I was recruited into the Moonies, I was instructed to suppress my moral objections to lying because it was for the greater good of bringing "Satan's children" back to God. This reprogramming of my conscience was meant to make me believe that lying was a form of love and spirituality.

REFLECTIVE EXERCISES

Use the following <u>Scientology video</u> to answer the following questions:

8. What persuasive techniques did you notice in the video?

_____

_____

_____

_____

_____

_____

_____

_____

_____

_____

9. Which of the four categories of Moonies recruitment does the video appeal to most?

_____

_____

_____

_____

_____

_____

_____

_____

_____

_____

10. How does Scientology establish credibility in its recruitment video to all four categories described in the Moonies recruitment tactic?

_____

_____

_____

_____

_____

_____

_____

_____

_____

_____

11. Do you think the video presents the image of being a cult? Why and why not?

_____

_____

_____

_____

_____

_____

_____

_____

_____

_____

12. Are there any red flags or warning signs you noticed in the video?

_____

_____

_____

_____
_____
_____
_____
_____
_____
_____
_____

13. Imagine you are speaking to someone, whether in a clinical or social setting, and they have just watched this video, mentioning its appeal to them. Name what you learned from this hypothetical discussion and then devise one or two tactics or strategies that can be used to help individuals resist the influence of the video?

_____
_____
_____
_____
_____
_____
_____
_____
_____
_____

As humans, we are motivated by two primary factors: the avoidance of negatives and the pursuit of positives, and it's important to have a balance of both. When it comes to leaving mind control cults, it's crucial for individuals to visualize a positive, fulfilling future. The goal is to empower them to be good citizens, consumers, and members of a greater community and to avoid getting involved in future harmful authoritarian cults.

MODULE 2 RESOURCES

Freedom of Mind Resources

How Cults Exploit Fervor and Awe to Recruit and Control Members

Authoritarian Bible Cults Actively Recruiting at College and Online

Asperger's/ Autism Spectrum Disorder and Undue Influence

Autism Extremism And Protecting The Vulnerable With Dr. Tony Attwood

UFOs, Anti-Government Conspiracy Theories, Covid-19, and Indoctrination

Social Media, Cyber Warfare, Data Mining and AI Used to Target, Manipulate and Control People

Rewired: Protecting Your Brain in the Digital Age

Books

Addiction as an Attachment Disorder by Philip J. Flores

Flores posits addiction stems from failed attachment relationships, advocating for interpersonal, relational treatment approaches to heal.

Thinking, Fast and Slow by Daniel Kahneman

Kahneman explores two modes of thought: intuitive, quick (System 1) and deliberative, slow (System 2), and their impact on decision-making.

MODULE 3: EXAMINING DESTRUCTIVE CULTS

Summary: Focuses on differentiating between destructive and benign cults, examining authoritarian control and mind control techniques.

Learning Objectives: Enable therapists to identify destructive cult practices and their effects, providing effective interventions for recovery.

As the <u>Influence Continuum</u> from Module 1 demonstrated, not all cults are destructive or authoritarian. There are ethical, benign, and even beneficial cults that provide transparency, open communication, and offer an easy exit if one wishes to do something else. Merely holding unconventional beliefs does not necessarily make a group a destructive cult.

A group becomes a destructive cult when it employs authoritarian tactics to control its members, utilizing influence to disrupt and replace their authentic identities with a new cult identity.

Destructive cults use deception and undue influence to create dependency and obedience. This approach leads to dissociative disorders and the disruption of personal goals, aspirations, and relationships. Such cults seek to control every aspect of a member's life, including their time and finances, to transform them into something else entirely. The root issue is the psychology of mind control, where the agenda is hidden or external to an individual's choices. Therefore, it's imperative to comprehend these destructive cults' workings and the associated risks before joining any group. There can be different strategies for working with someone in a religious cult than someone in a therapy or political cult.

I have witnessed, especially since the COVID-19 pandemic, that more authoritarian cults are recruiting online. Some cults buy user data from companies and use this data to target vulnerable people. They may recruit through video gaming platforms, dating and hookup sites, porn sites, and hypnosis sites, as well as through popular social media such as TikTok, Instagram and X (formerly Twitter). There are also encrypted messaging platforms that a targeted person might be invited to join to keep their family and friends from knowing anything about their activities.

Recruitment into a destructive cult often involves isolating as well as indoctrinating the new member. This can be overwhelming and exhausting due to the new time and work commitments. Conflict with family and friends as well as inner turmoil can worsen these effects.

THE PYRAMID STRUCTURE OF DESTRUCTIVE CULTS

As outlined in Module 1, destructive cults typically have an <u>authoritarian pyramid structure</u> with the cult leader as the head and sub-leaders, followed by core devotees and rank-and-file members below.

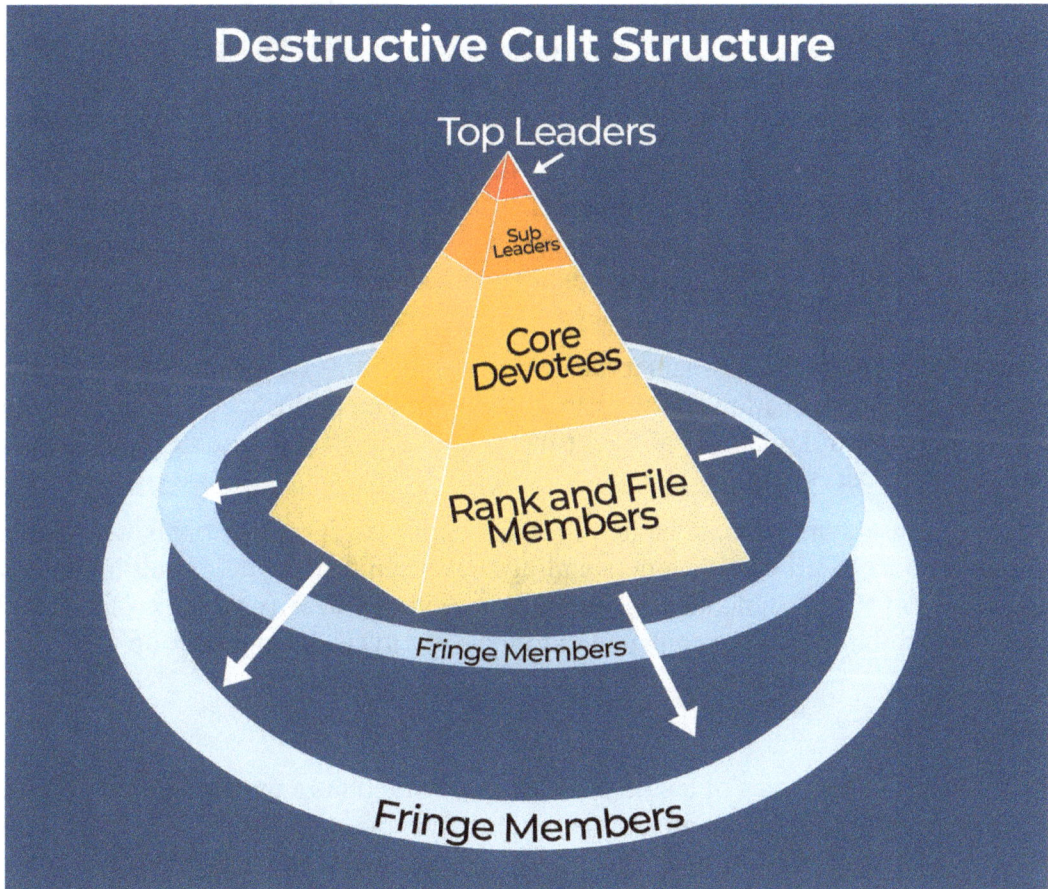

Destructive Cult Structure

Top Leaders
Sub Leaders
Core Devotees
Rank and File Members
Fringe Members
Fringe Members

Finally, on the outskirts are the fringe members, who are not exposed to the cult's inner workings. Understanding the pyramid structure allows for a more nuanced analysis of one's involvements and investment in a cult. This concept is therefore essential for therapists to explain to clients as a psychoeducational tool, one of many that can equip individuals to identify and/or resist undue influence

When evaluating a former cult member, it can be beneficial to start from the beginning of their affiliation and identify their position within the organization, such as whether they were born into the group and/or in leadership roles within the hierarchy.

Higher-ranking members may be the only ones privy to inner teachings and secrets, and peripheral members may only receive limited information from recruiters.

For example, Scientology operates on a pay-per-level system, with the most exclusive teachings (the Operating Thetan [OT] levels) accessible only to those who pay substantial sums of money or sign a contract to work for years.

Former members and fringe members of Transcendental Meditation (TM) often need to be made aware of the mantra fraud. In TM, followers are told they are being given a mantra. They are told to keep it secret, as it is individualized for them only. The reality is that there is a chart of mantras depending on the person's age and the year they were initiated.

When I meet people who tell me they did TM decades ago but no longer do it, I sometimes ask them what their mantra is. When they say they can't tell me, I ask "why not?" They say they aren't supposed to tell anyone. Then, if they are still unwilling to state their mantra I ask them how old they were when they joined and what year, look it up, and tell them, and they are so shocked. Then, they are open to hearing they were defrauded.

It is also common for cult members to be demoted or become fringe members, impacting their access to information and their level of involvement. Fringe members may be unaware of the harmful practices of the group as they are not privy to the group's deeper hierarchy and practices.

Recognizing these dynamics can be helpful for mental health professionals when assessing clients who have left a cult. Understanding the pyramid structure of cult involvement can help clients to understand their experiences better and identify patterns of manipulation and control that may have contributed to their involvement in the group.

TYPES OF CULTS

When asked about their idea of a cult, most people will conjure up the image of a group of religious devotees following an alternative doctrine and worshiping an authoritarian leader. Many cults fit into this category, but destructive cults take many forms.

Mind control and undue influence can also be present in political groups, self-help groups, large group awareness training groups, multi-level marketing organizations, authoritarian families, controlling relationships, labor and sex trafficking, and conspiracy groups.

POLITICAL CULTS

Political cults are typically characterized by an authoritarian structure with a leader who desires to maintain power indefinitely, often through brutal and repressive tactics. These regimes often silence critics and dissidents through imprisonment, violence, or even death. For instance, China's cruel treatment of Uyghur Muslims involves efforts to assimilate them into mainstream Chinese culture while destroying their cultural identity. Political cults also control the media, limit protests and free assembly, and manipulate elections to maintain power. For example, Putin has no tolerance for anyone he believes is a threat or who has challenged his power.

It is important to remember that modern day political regimes might want to maintain an appearance of being democratic and open to opposition as a form of psychological warfare. These tactics may include planting faux opposition candidates and allowing a degree of freedom in the press, in part to say, "Look, I'm not authoritarian."

In the case of Russia, "active measures" are used as a tactic. "Active measures" refer to Soviet and Russian security services' tactics for political warfare and global influence. These include disinformation, propaganda to manipulate public opinion, psychological operations to alter perceptions, and covert political influence operations aimed at swaying political outcomes. Originally part of Soviet intelligence doctrine, these strategies involve a mix of media manipulation and actions with varying degrees of violence, targeting both international and domestic spheres.

Many "mainstream" political organizations, on the left and the right, meet the criteria of a harmful cult. For example, in my book, *The Cult of Trump*, I explain how Donald Trump employs many of the same techniques as prominent cult leaders — lying, insulting opponents, sowing fear and confusion, demanding absolute loyalty, shunning and belittling critics and former supporters, and distracting and presenting competing versions of reality to confuse and coerce his followers.

Political cults can take on the guise of a religion, but their goals and actions are typically politically motivated. Additionally, political cults may include terrorist groups that target and kill innocent civilians or lone actors who carry out acts of terror.

Terrorist organizations can be state-run or operated by cult groups. They use various cult tactics outlined in my BITE Model, including deception, manipulation, isolation from friends and family, and love bombing. Members of terrorist groups employ black-and-white thinking and often only associate with others who share the same ideology and beliefs.

Like in any other cult, members of violent extremist groups are deceptively recruited and indoctrinated. In an increasingly digital world, much of this recruitment takes place online on social media. First, recruiters target people who "like" specific posts on social media and build rapport with them. Then, recruiters use manipulative tactics to draw people deeper into the group.

A well-known example of a terrorist group is ISIS/DAESH, which is recognized as an extremist Islamic organization. They are known for brutal executions of Western journalists, suicide bombings, and violence against those who don't subscribe to their beliefs. The group operates as a mind control cult that uses manipulative tactics bolstering its extreme religious convictions. Using fear and intimidation, ISIS/DAESH promotes a distorted and violent interpretation of Islam to recruit and exert control over its followers. Members are subjected to strict rules and expected to submit to the leader's authority. The group employs brainwashing and mind control strategies to retain power over its members, compelling them to commit heinous terrorist attacks and violent acts. The Muslim community widely condemns ISIS/DAESH, viewing it as a deviant and dangerous group that misrepresents the actual teachings of Islam.

RELIGIOUS/SPIRITUAL CULTS

Religious or spiritual cults are focused on religious dogma. Some groups, such as those rooted in scripture (Jewish, Muslim, Christian), have leaders who claim to be a messiah, a prophet, or an apostle. Other groups based on Eastern religion (Hindu, Buddhist, Sikh) have leaders who claim to be enlightened avatars, gurus, or masters. The idea that one must surrender to an enlightened master or guru and obey them can be very harmful.

Doomsday cults, like the World Mission Society Church of God (WMSCOG), Worldwide Church of God, and Heaven's Gate, are apocalyptic and believe that the end of the world is near. They discourage their members from having children or pursuing education and often ignore ecological concerns in direct connection to their belief that the end is near.

These groups believe in "purifying" the world (by their definition) and getting rid of all sin. They often promise that the world will be magically recreated. Some doomsday cults set a specific time for the end of the world to maximize their members' work and financial contributions while the leader(s) live in luxury.

Pagan and neo-pagan group leaders claim to be masters of the occult. Some religious Christians may view them as satanic, although they do not believe in Satan, and most of these groups are harmless. They have an organic and nature-based approach, using herbs and celebrating seasonal worship. However, some pagan and neo-pagan groups exhibit destructive cult characteristics.

Therapists benefit from learning about one group in each category as a foundation. Then, compare as you learn about more groups. Over time, you can develop an extensive library of resources and gain confidence in working with this client population. Learning the language and understanding the beliefs in this field are essential.

SELF-HELP OR PSEUDO-THERAPY CULTS

Self-help and pseudo-therapy cults can be a single therapist and their client(s), or a group of therapists who organize workshops and seminars. They use self-improvement and counseling to target people and corporations, claiming you will succeed by taking their courses and seminars.

Unfortunately, many unqualified coaches have no formal ethical standards or mental health training, making it easier for such cults to arise. In some cases, individuals previously part of a cult may splinter off and create their own cult. Therapists who engage in unethical behavior can exploit clients in various ways, such as isolating them from their loved ones, exploiting them financially, sexually abusing them, or fostering dependency rather than empowering them. Therefore, it is crucial for therapists to be mindful of their own beliefs and to maintain a humble, curious, and open attitude. Seeking ongoing learning and growth is valuable.

LARGE GROUP AWARENESS TRAINING

Large Group Awareness Training (LGAT) programs, such as Lifespring and Erhard Seminars Training (est), gained popularity in the 1970s, with individuals paying substantial fees to attend mass seminars. Warner Erhard, formerly Jack Rosenberg, was a prominent figure in the mass training movement. The Landmark Forum, a successor to est, also emerged along with The Hunger Project as a spin-off project that said it could combat hunger by enrolling more people into the group.

LGATs often use hypnotic visualizations, hype, public confrontation using curse words and shock techniques, and various other psychological methods to induce "high experiences" and altered states of consciousness.

Through high-pressure tactics, recruiters encourage individuals to sign up for costly workshops that promise transformation, enlightenment, or wealth-building strategies. Coaches promise personal transformation but are not trained mental health professionals. Nor is there any sufficient screening done ahead of time to determine if a person is too unstable or at too fragile a point in their lives to attend. Typically, the recruiters keep the program's details secret to avoid 'spoiling' the experience. While some individuals initially have positive experiences, many report diminishing returns over time.

To understand one of the most financially successful transformation groups, watch Netflix's Tony Robbins: I am Not Your Guru. Robbins learned Neuro-Linguistic Programming (NLP) and reportedly made a financial arrangement with the creators of NLP—John Grinder and Richard Bandler—to use it without attributing it to another source.

Robbins knows the power of hypnosis. In one scene in the documentary, he tells a former Children of God cult member, "I am not your guru," only to later offer to "mentor" her.

Some LGATs program the idea in the people attending that they are like gods, have mastery over their destiny, and "create their reality." This belief system suggests that there are no accidents or coincidences in the universe and that one must look into one's soul to understand why one created specific negative experiences for oneself.

LGATs can feel electrifying and transformative in the moment, but beneath the hype and pressure lies a system that exploits vulnerability, often leaving individuals emotionally drained and signing up for the next program. There is often significant pressure to recruit others to attend.

For instance, if someone was raped, they may be told to explore why they needed to create that experience for themselves, negating the concept of victimhood and asserting that individuals choose everything that happens to them. However, without ongoing informed consent, individuals cannot agree ahead of time to unknown requests or beliefs that may be presented when their critical thinking is compromised.

REFLECTIVE EXERCISES

Use the Netflix Trailer of _Tony Robbins: I Am Not Your Guru_ to answer the following questions:

1.   What techniques do you observe Tony Robbins using to influence and control the behavior of participants?

_____

_____

_____

_____

_____

_____

_____

_____

2.   What are the potential psychological and emotional risks for participants who may be vulnerable to manipulation or have a history of trauma?

_____

_____

_____

_____

_____

_____

_____

_____

_____

_____

MULTI-LEVEL MARKETING CULTS

Multi-level marketing groups (MLMs) are pyramid-shaped marketing organizations. The focus is on recruiting people to recruit others, presumably giving a cut of the income up the chain. Examples include Amway, Herbalife, Mary Kay, LuLaRoe, and doTERRA-convicted trafficker Keith Raniere. (For example, Keith Raniere had been ordered never to run an MLM by 20 Attorney Generals for his work in the company Consumers Buyline. To avoid scrutiny, he had Nancy Saltzman front the coaching MLM for him. She went to jail, too.)

Most MLMs use deceptive recruitment, financial manipulation, and the promise of large profits. They exploit people's aspirations for wealth and financial freedom by portraying traditional employment as enslavement. These groups argue that true freedom can only be attained through entrepreneurial independence rather than working for others. MLMs tend to exaggerate success stories and encourage people by saying they can work part-time, earn millions, and retire early. Most people who join MLMs lose money by paying for expensive workshops, courses, seminars, and/or inventory.

Recruiters are very convincing. They use deception using classic cult recruitment techniques (withholding vital information, distorting information, and outright lying) to trap people who have not learned about cult mind control techniques.

Amway is among the largest and most prominent multi-level marketing cults, with hundreds of millions of dollars in fines due to their deceptive practices. Yet, despite these fines, the organization continues to operate and thrive because the profits generated by these cults outweigh the potential costs of legal penalties.

HUMAN TRAFFICKING

Human trafficking uses force, fraud, or coercion to exploit people for labor, slavery, or commercial sex. It is illegal in most countries, including the United States. Unfortunately, traffickers are using the internet to target vulnerable young people, grooming them for pornography, prostitution, and other forms of exploitation. Once they are under the control of the traffickers, their situation can quickly escalate and become much worse.

Perpetrators may use psychological manipulation tactics to control and exploit their victims, including isolation, physical and emotional abuse, threats, and coercion. In some cases, traffickers may also use drugs or other substances to control their victims' behavior and create a state of dependency. This action can make it more difficult for victims to leave or seek help, as they may fear the consequences of doing so or feel that they cannot survive on their own.

Mind control techniques are often used to establish power and control over trafficking victims, making it more difficult for them to escape or seek help from law enforcement or other authorities. As such, addressing the issue of human trafficking often involves physical intervention, rescue efforts, and psychological support for victims to help them recover from the trauma of their experiences.

Biderman's Framework, also known as the "Chart of Coercion," is a model developed by Albert Biderman in the 1950s to explain the methods used to extract false confessions from prisoners of war during the Korean War.

While the model was not explicitly designed to address trafficking, it has been used to study the tactics used by traffickers to control and manipulate their victims. Biderman's Framework includes eight tactics of coercion that can be used to break down an individual's resistance and force compliance. These tactics include isolation, monopolization of perception, induced debility and exhaustion, threats, occasional indulgences, demonstrating "omnipotence," degradation, and enforcing trivial demands.

Traffickers may use one or more of these tactics to control their victims, making it difficult for them to resist or escape. By understanding these tactics, advocates in fields like law enforcement and mental health can better recognize the signs of trafficking and work to support victims in breaking free from their captors. Trafficking experts also use my BITE Model to identify and understand the specific behaviors of coercion.

Sex traffickers create psychological chains by:

- Taking advantage of their victim's vulnerability;
- Depriving them of basic needs;
- Creating an environment of fear;
- Employing confusion and unpredictability;
- Breaking down self-esteem;
- Prohibiting free will;
- Moving their victim to an unfamiliar place or country so they are isolated;
- Instilling learned helplessness, and
- Inducing punishment, such as branding, torturing, raping, and other forms of violence.

Some traffickers even impregnate their victims, making exiting the situation even more challenging. Women who have children by rape may struggle to bond with their children due to their resemblance to their abuser. Additionally, pimps may use technology such as smartphones to monitor the movements and earnings of their victims, further compounding the victim's sense of helplessness and lack of control.

Pimpin' Ken, whose real name is Ken Ivy, is an American author and former pimp known for his book *Pimpology: The 48 Laws of the Game*. The book is a memoir that provides a disturbing guide for those interested in becoming successful pimps. It outlines the rules of the "game" and includes advice on controlling and manipulating women for financial gain.

Ending The Game is a "coercion resiliency" curriculum that reduces feelings of attachment to traffickers and a lifestyle characterized by commercial sexual exploitation, thereby reducing the rate of recidivism among sex trafficking victims. The curriculum is designed to educate and empower commercial sex trafficking victims by providing a framework to uncover harmful psychological coercion (aka "The Game") that victims have been subjected to with their trafficking experience. By revealing a sequence of commonly used, yet seldom-explained mind control techniques used by traffickers, sexual abusers, media, and other coercive agents, the aim is to empower victims to acquire skills and end "The Game."

MINI-CULTS

Mini-cults are cults with fewer than ten people. Often, there is a power differential between the abuser and the abused in mini-cults. For example, the abuser may be a parent, teacher, therapist, boss, coach, or religious leader. In addition, mini cults can be a splinter group of a former cult.

An example of a mini-cult is the Lawrence Ray cult, featured on Hulu's three-part docuseries *Stolen Youth*. Lawrence Ray is a financial fraudster and the father of a former Sarah Lawrence College student who brainwashed and manipulated several of his daughter's peers, including demanding that they participate in "therapy sessions," in which he sexually, physically, and emotionally abused them. He also reportedly extorted large sums of money from them and forced them into illegal activities. After his arrest in 2020, several victims shared their stories, describing the cult-like atmosphere he created and the psychological damage they suffered due to his abuse. On January 20th, 2023, Larry Ray was sentenced to 60 years in prison for a racketeering conspiracy, violent crime in aid of racketeering, extortion, sex trafficking, forced labor, tax evasion, and money laundering offenses.

I was involved in a follow-up episode to the series "Stolen Youth," premiered on Hulu, focusing on the recovery of cult survivors. On Hulu, search for "Impact x Nightline" and look for the "Stolen Youth" episode. I sat and talked with Daniel Levin—whom I interviewed in a blog on freedomofmind.com—and MD Felicia Rosario.

FAMILY CULTS

Family cults are authoritarian and use the methods outlined in the BITE Model to run the household and raise children to be dependent and obedient. In this model, the family is the primary unit of control and manipulation.

Usually, the parents want to keep their children in a child-like state of obedience, no matter what. Strict rules, high demands, and little responsiveness or warmth characterize authoritarian parenting. Parents who use this style tend to have high expectations of their children but provide little emotional support or open communication. They tend to be inflexible and punitive and may rely heavily on physical punishment or shaming to discipline their children.

Authoritative parenting, on the other hand, is a healthier style characterized by setting clear and reasonable expectations for children while being responsive to their needs and feelings. Parents who use this approach set limits for their children while encouraging independence and individuality. In addition, they often use positive reinforcement and reasoning to guide behavior and help their children understand the reasons behind rules and consequences.

When I help people raised in authoritarian households, including religious cults, a necessary component is teaching them what a family is supposed to act like.

ONE-ON-ONE CULTS

One-on-one cults involve a power differential in which one person dominates the other. This can occur in various situations, including controlling relationships, elderly abuse, and other forms of domestic abuse. In these situations, the dominant person may use manipulation, gaslighting, or physical violence to control the other person. One-on-one cults can be particularly insidious, as the person being controlled may not even realize they are being manipulated or abused.

In 2014, California updated the definition of undue influence to mean excessive persuasion that causes another person to act or refrain from acting by overcoming that person's free will and results in inequity. In determining whether a result was produced by undue influence, all of the following factors are considered:

1. Vulnerability of the victim (e.g., cognitive impairment, illness, disability, injury, emotional distress, isolation, or dependency).

2. Influencer's source of power or authority (e.g., family member, care provider, health care professional, legal professional, or expert).

3. Unfair actions or tactics used by the influencer.

4. Evidence of an unfair or inequitable result.

The law includes a legal provision to protect vulnerable elderly individuals from being taken advantage of by those who use undue influence to gain control over them or their assets. Under this law, if it can be proven that someone used excessive persuasion or coercion to convince an older person to make a particular decision, the court can invalidate any legal document created due to that influence. This includes wills, trusts, and other financial documents. The law is intended to prevent elder abuse and exploitation and ensure that the older person's wishes are respected and protected.

CONSPIRACY THEORY CULTS

Conspiracy theory cults are groups that promote and follow conspiracy theories, such as the existence of secret societies or government cover-ups. They may engage in fear mongering, propaganda, or isolation from mainstream society.

During times of social uncertainty and collective trauma, the prevalence of conspiracy theories increases. People are more susceptible to those who offer certainty when society is undergoing stressors. During such times, individuals are often searching for hope and answers. Moreover, studies have found that if someone confidently declares an erroneous fact, it is more likely to be believed if it is more outrageous than "believable". In addition, researchers have found that individuals who subscribe to conspiracies are more likely to interpret nonsensical statements as profound.

- *Lyndon LaRouche* — LaRouche was an American political activist, writer, and founder of the LaRouche movement. He ran for President of the United States eight times, beginning in 1976. He was antisemitic and a conspiracist. LaRouche's views were controversial and often considered far right and fringe, and his organization was accused of being a cult. He was convicted of federal fraud and conspiracy charges in 1988 and served a prison sentence. LaRouche died in 2019, but the cult continues to function. LaRouche was a friend of Roger Stone and Russia.

- *L. Ron Hubbard* — Hubbard, the founder of Scientology, has promoted many controversial beliefs. According to his teachings, "Xenu" was a galactic dictator who brought billions of people to Earth in spacecraft 75 million years ago, stacked them around volcanoes, and then destroyed them using hydrogen bombs, thereby releasing thetans (immortal spirits) that attached themselves to humans and caused them spiritual harm. The "Wall of Fire" refers to a barrier that allegedly surrounds the Earth and prevents people from achieving spiritual freedom, which can only be achieved through Scientology practices.

- *David Icke* — David Icke is an English writer, speaker, and conspiracist with a significant following. He promotes conspiracy theories, including believing in a New World Order controlling the world and a cabal of shape-shifting reptilian aliens who rule the planet. He has also claimed that the moon is a hollowed-out planetoid.

- *Plandemic* - "Plandemic" is a conspiracy documentary video that went viral in May 2020, spreading various misinformation about the COVID-19 pandemic. The video makes several false claims about the origins of the virus and the actions of governments, pharmaceutical companies, and other organizations in response to it. The video was widely debunked by fact-checkers and public health experts, who highlighted the many inaccuracies and misleading claims made in the film.

REFLECTIVE EXERCISES

3. Select any types of cults or unhealthy groups you have been personally involved in or have heard of:

☐   ☐   ☐

Political cult   Religious/spiritual cult   Self-help/Pseudo-therapy cult

☐   ☐   ☐

One-on-one cult   Conspiracy cult   Large group awareness training

☐   ☐   ☐

Mini cult   Family cult   Multi-level marketing cult

☐

Human trafficking

4. Refer to the Influence Continuum in Module 1 and reflect on what made the above group(s) unhealthy. Write down your insights.

_____

_____

_____

_____

_____

_____
_____
_____
_____
_____

5. If you are a mental health professional, select any of the types of cults or unhealthy groups you have encountered among your clients:

☐   ☐   ☐
Political cult   Religious/spiritual cult   Self-Help/Pseudo-Therapy Cults

☐   ☐   ☐
One-on-one cult   Conspiracy cult   Large Group Awareness
                                                  Training

☐   ☐   ☐
Mini cult   Family cult   Multi-level marketing cult

☐
Human Trafficking

Other: _____

6. From what your client shared, what factors helped you identify this group as a cult or unhealthy group?

_____
_____
_____
_____
_____
_____
_____
_____
_____

CLINICIANS ARE NOT IMMUNE

The myth of invulnerability is a misconception among therapists who believe their clients cannot unduly influence them. Unfortunately, therapists are susceptible to mind control and undue influence, as evidenced by multiple cases of untrained therapists falling under the influence of clients with a dissociative identity disorder. That is, the therapist was so-ciocognitively influenced to believe they also had the disorder. To prevent this, therapists must be trained to identify dissociative disorders and obtain adequate supervision.

Indeed, therapists have been known to be recruited into cults, with recruiters encouraging members to seek therapy from these therapists. In addition, some therapists have been involved in multi-level marketing cults where they attempt to sell products to their clients. To prevent such situations, therapists must establish and maintain clear boundaries, avoiding dual relationships with clients.

Therapists must not have a religious agenda to persuade their clients to leave a cult and adopt a specific faith, whether Christianity, Judaism, or Islam. Clients recovering from the effects of mind control cults are highly vulnerable, and it is the therapist's role to em-power them by providing tools and psychoeducation, not by imposing their beliefs.

THE PROFILE OF A CULT LEADER: MALIGNANT NARCISSISM

Narcissism is a personality trait characterized by a grandiose sense of self-importance, a sense of entitlement, a lack of empathy, and a need for admiration. Narcissists have an inflated view of their abilities and achievements and often believe they are superior to others. As a result, they may seek constant praise and admiration and tend to exploit others for their own gain.

Although not included in the DSM as a specific classification, malignant narcissism is a psychological term for severe narcissistic personality disorder. Psychoanalyst Erich Fromm introduced the term in 1964, but psychologist and psychoanalyst Otto Kernberg further developed it in the 1980s.

Narcissism exists on a continuum. On the healthier end are narcissists who have a high sense of themselves, but they can take criticism, apologize and mean it, and be capable of more self-reflection. On the unhealthy end of the spectrum is narcissistic personality disorder, which is included in the Diagnostic and Statistical Manual of Mental Disorders (DSM-V-TR), in which narcissistic traits cause significant impairment in social, occupational, or other areas of functioning.

Narcissistic Personality Disorder (NPD) often fuels grandiose fantasies of success, admiration, and power, masking deep insecurity and a need for constant validation from others.

Charismatic and highly-skilled at creating a cult-like following, malignant narcissists use their power and control to influence others. Numerous cult leaders, including Jim Jones, L. Ron Hubbard, and Sun Myung Moon, have been identified as malignant narcissists. In my book, _The Cult of Trump_, I demonstrate how <u>Donald Trump exhibits the traits of a malignant narcissist</u>.

These traits include:

- Self-centered behavior
- Fantasies of power and success, and attractiveness
- A need for praise and admiration
- A sense of entitlement
- Lack of empathy and antisocial behavior
- Pathological lying
- Interpersonally exploitative behavior
- Sadism, harassment and silencing
- Violence, and paranoia.

They believe they are superior, and people are in the world for their beck and call. They also believe they cannot trust friends, allies, associates, or subordinates—no matter how close. The individual is highly prone to seeing others as objects to be used or destroyed rather than human beings with their own needs and desires.

CASE STUDY: MARSHALL APPLEWHITE/ HEAVEN'S GATE

Marshall Applewhite was an American cult leader who founded the Heaven's Gate group in the 1970s. He was born in 1931, in Texas, and had a troubled childhood due to his father's alcoholism, financial difficulties, and religious homophobia. Applewhite married in the early 1950s and initially pursued a career in music at the University of Alabama, but lost his position after it was discovered he was having an affair with a male student. Applewhite went through a divorce in 1968 and faced rejection from his father after disclosing his homosexuality to his parents. Following his departure from the University of Alabama, Applewhite assumed the position of music department chair at the University of St. Thomas in Houston, Texas. However, in 1970, he resigned from this post, citing emotional turmoil.

In the early 1970s, Applewhite became increasingly interested in spirituality and UFOs. He started teaching a course at a community college, where he met Bonnie Nettles, a nurse interested in theosophy, who recruited him to be her co-leader in the cult, whose final name was Heaven's Gate.

In 1975, Applewhite was imprisoned for six months for failing to return a rental car, which he believed he was "divinely authorized" to keep. During his time in jail, he continued to develop his religious beliefs. Following Applewhite's release from prison, he and Nettles committed to establishing contact with extraterrestrial beings and recruiting individuals who shared their beliefs.

Applewhite and Nettles, who also went by the "spiritual" names of Do and Ti, respectively, believed they were messengers of extraterrestrial beings and had a special mission to prepare their followers for an impending apocalypse. They taught their followers that the only way to survive the world's end was to leave their earthly bodies and ascend to a higher plane of existence. To achieve this, members of Heaven's Gate were told to sever ties with friends, family, media, cease using drugs, stop drinking alcohol, stop wearing jewelry, renounce facial hair, eschew all forms of sexuality and show total devotion to Applewhite and Nettles. To assess the loyalty of their followers, Applewhite and Nettles once instructed them to wait outside all night in anticipation of a visit from extraterrestrial beings. However, they later revealed that this was merely a test of their followers' commitment.

In 1985, Nettles died of cancer, leaving Applewhite distraught and questioning his belief in physical ascension. He informed the group that Nettles had left her physical form behind to embark on a journey to the "Next Level" because she had "too much energy to remain on Earth." Applewhite stated that Nettles had advanced to a higher spiritual plane than himself, which was why she had abandoned him. Applewhite began to refer to Nettles as "the Father" and used male pronouns while referring to her.

Applewhite became increasingly paranoid and fearful of a conspiracy against his group. He began to increasingly discuss the Apocalypse, comparing the Earth to an overgrown garden that was to be recycled or "spaded under." In the early 1990s, the number of members in the group decreased significantly, giving Applewhite a sense of urgency. By 1996, he talked about the impending arrival of Comet Hale-Bopp and an accompanying spaceship, which would transport them to a different planet where their spirits would be received.

Tragically, in 1997, Applewhite convinced 39 of his followers to commit mass suicide by ingesting a lethal cocktail of drugs and placing bags over their heads. They had been told the spacecraft would take them to reach the "next level" of existence. The group's suicide was carefully planned and orchestrated, with members donning matching outfits with patches that read "Heaven's Gate Away Team."

REFLECTIVE EXERCISES

Watch the following <u>video of Marshall Applewhite</u> made shortly before the mass suicide:

7. What narcissistic traits does Marshall Applewhite demonstrate?

_____

_____

_____

_____

_____

_____

_____

_____

_____

_____

8. In what ways did the Heaven's Gate cult exhibit the characteristics of a destructive cult, as defined by my BITE Model?

_____

_____

_____

_____

_____

_____

_____

_____

_____

_____

_____

CULT LEADER EXAMPLES

For mental health professionals looking to help clients recover from the influence of a mind control cult, it is essential to have familiarity with some of the most well-known cults and cult leaders, both from the past and present. The following are major figures:

CHARLES MANSON

Charles Manson (1934 — 2017) was a notorious cult leader who formed a group known as the Manson Family in the late 1960s. Manson's manipulation and brainwashing of his followers led them to commit brutal murders, including the infamous Tate-LaBianca murders in 1969. Manson's cult was marked by his charismatic personality, apocalyptic beliefs, and use of drugs and music to influence his followers. Manson had over 150 hours of Scientology programming, which no doubt helped arm him to hypnotize his followers.

Despite his attempts to portray himself as a countercultural figure, Manson's actions ultimately revealed him to be a violent and manipulative cult leader who caused immense harm to those under his influence. Manson died in 2017, while serving a life sentence in prison. Several members of his cult remain incarcerated and have long since expressed remorse for their actions.

JIM JONES

Jim Jones (1932 — 1978) was a cult leader who founded the People's Temple in 1955. Jones created a religious community based on a mix of socialism, communism, and Christianity. His followers believed that he was a prophet, and he used that belief to control them. In 1978, Jones ordered the assassination of Congressman Leo J. Ryan when he flew to Guyana to see if people were being held against their will. This effort led over 900 of his followers to die by drinking cyanide-laced Flavor Aid or be shot. The event, known as the Jonestown Massacre, was one of the largest mass murders of Americans in history.

Jones's actions and the tragedy that resulted from them continue to serve as a stark reminder of the dangers of charismatic leaders who seek to manipulate and control their followers. Senator Robert Dole invited me to Washington, DC to speak about cults following this tragedy. Unfortunately, cult lobbying got me and a former People's Temple member taken off the speaking agenda.

DAVID KORESH

David Koresh was an American cult leader and founder of the Branch Davidians, a sect that believed in an imminent apocalypse. He was born Vernon Howell in Houston, Texas, in 1959, and assumed the name David Koresh after claiming to be a prophet. In 1993, a tragic event unfolded when the FBI and ATF raided the Branch Davidian compound in Waco, Texas. The initial gunfight and 51-day standoff resulted in violence. The FBI sent tanks to use gas on the cult members. This resulted in a fire that engulfed the compound, ultimately leading to the deaths of Koresh and 76 of his followers. Many anti-government individuals use the tragedy at Waco as a rallying cry to civil war.

BHAGWAN SHREE RAJNEESH

Bhagwan Shree Rajneesh (OSHO) was an Indian sex guru and cult leader who gained a significant following in India in the 1970s before moving to the United States in the 1980s. He founded a community called Rajneeshpuram in Oregon that was involved in criminal activity, including wiretapping and immigration fraud. In 1984, his followers committed a bioterrorism attack by contaminating salad bars in local restaurants with salmonella to influence the outcome of an upcoming election and prevent non-cult members from voting. Over 750 people fell ill from the attack. Fortunately, no one died.

His community was notorious for its drug use, sex practices, forced abortions, and sterilization of women. Rajneesh eventually pleaded guilty to immigration fraud and fled the country with several top aides to avoid charges related to the bioterror attack and other crimes. Rajneesh died in 1990. However, the cult continues using the name Osho as a rebrand.

RON HUBBARD

Ron Hubbard was an American author, occultist, and the founder of Scientology. He was born in 1911 in Nebraska, and grew up in Montana. In the 1930s, he began writing science fiction and fantasy stories and became a prolific pulp fiction writer. In 1950, he published *Dianetics: The Modern Science of Mental Health*, which became the basis for the Church of Scientology. The cult of Scientology has since grown to become a highly controversial organization with claims of millions of followers worldwide. Hubbard died in 1986, and David Miscavige staged a coup to take over.

Formerly the third-highest-ranking member of the international organization, 46-year member and previous director of OSA (Office of Special Affairs, essentially Scientology's version of the Gestapo), Mike Rinder departed from the cult. He has since collaborated with actress Leah Remini on a TV show that originally aired on A&E and is now available on other platforms. Together, they host a podcast aimed at exposing the facts about the cult's atrocities.

TONY ALAMO

Tony Alamo (birth name Bernie LaZar Hoffman) was a notoriously anti-Catholic, anti-gay, polygamous cult leader and the founder of Tony Alamo Christian Ministries. He was also a child sex offender. On September 20th, 2008, federal and state agents raided his headquarters with allegations of abuses. He was found guilty in 2009 on all federal counts of physical and sexual abuse, polygamy, and underage marriage. He was sentenced to 175 years in prison. He remained in jail until his death in May 2017.

KEITH RANIERE

Keith Raniere is the founder of the NXIVM cult. He operated a multi-level marketing cult called Consumers' Buyline, which 20 U.S. Attorney Generals shut down. Raniere co-founded NXIVM with Nancy Salzman in 1998. The organization offered personal and professional development courses through its Executive Success Program (ESP). NXIVM claimed to help people achieve their full potential and become more successful personally and professionally. However, former group members accused Raniere of engaging in sexual misconduct and abusive and coercive behavior, including branding women with his initials. In 2018, Raniere was arrested and charged with a range of crimes, including sex trafficking, forced labor, and conspiracy. Several other members of the organization, including Nancy Salzman, were sentenced to prison.

MICHAEL W. FINE

Michael W. Fine is a former divorce attorney convicted of using hypnosis to rape his clients. Fine preyed on vulnerable women who were going through a divorce, telling them he could teach them a relaxation technique to alleviate their stress. He would then hypnotize and sexually assault them, leaving them with amnesia about his unethical behavior. He was arrested in 1994 after several women came forward with accusations of sexual assault, and an investigation was launched, eventually leading to his arrest. Fine was subsequently convicted of sexual assault and sentenced to 12 years in prison.

While not all cult groups are harmful, it's essential to be aware of the signs and tactics of destructive cults. These groups employ authoritarian tactics to control and manipulate their members through mind control techniques. Destructive cults can take many forms, including political, religious, self-help, multi-level marketing, and even conspiracy theory cults. To avoid falling victim to a harmful cult and help former members recover, it's crucial to understand these groups' workings and the associated risks.

Malignant narcissism can play a significant role in the behavior of cult leaders and may lead to destructive and violent behavior toward their followers. Therefore, awareness and education are vital to avoid the dangers of destructive cults and maintain personal autonomy and control over one's life.

MODULE 3 RESOURCES

Freedom of Mind Resources

Beware of Political Cult Groups that Manipulate and Control Members

Political Cults, Leadership, Idealism, and Totalism: A Discussion with Dennis Tourish, PhD.

Malcolm Nance: Terrorists are Cult Members Who Do Violence

Violent Extremism: Best Practices for Prevention and Rehabilitation of Terrorists

Lone-Actor Terrorism: An Integrated Framework

Scientology and the BITE Model

Growing Up in Scientology and the Aftermath Foundation with Aaron Smith-Levin

A Billion Years: My Escape From a Life in the Highest Ranks of Scientology with Mike Rinder

My Appearance on Leah Remini: Scientology and the Aftermath, and Other Updates

Transcendental Meditation (TM) and Re-Evaluation Counseling in Schools

Escaping Transcendental Meditation: Nurse Midwife Gina Catena Tells Her Story

Growing up in an Apocalyptic Cult: A conversation with Dr. Tricia Jenkins

Multi-Level Marketing and Self-Help Cult Groups: Learn the Warning Signs

LuLaRoe and the World of Commercial Cults: Interview With Roberta Blevins

Talking MLMs with Douglas Brooks

Beware the "Main Street Bubble" of Multi-Level Marketing Groups Without U.S. Government Protection

Questionable Legislation Sponsored to Make Pyramid Schemes Legal

Multi-Level Marketing Groups Defraud Consumers!

Human Trafficking

Combating Human Trafficking—A Conversation with Paul Chang

Human Trafficking — Survivor Voices are Critical: A Conversation with a Survivor, Attorney Carissa Phelps

Healing From Torture and Human Trafficking

Human Trafficking: Learn to Recognize the Signs and Help Save a Life

Sex and Labor Trafficking Awareness, Survivor Empowerment, and Saving Children From Abuse: A Discussion With Rachel Thomas, MEd.

One-on-One Cults — How Coercive Control Made Sarma Melngailis the Bad Vegan

Conspiracy Theories, Cults and How to Help Friends and Loved Ones with Debunker Mick West

Conspiracy Theories: Their Origin, Effect and How to Debunk Them with Mick West

The Allure of Conspiracy Theories and How to Dispel Them with Dr. Michael Shermer

UFOs, Anti-Government Conspiracy Theories, Covid-19, and Indoctrination With Author and Journalist M.J. Banias

QAnon: What Is It About? A Discussion With Conspiracy Theory Researcher Travis View

Malignant Narcissism: Stereotypical Characteristics of a Cult Leader

Donald Trump, Cults and Narcissism: A Discussion with Sociologist Dr. Stephen Kent

Hubbard, Trump, and Narcissism: A Discussion with Jon Atack

Donald Trump and Narcissism

Traumatic Narcissism: From Muktananda and Gurumayi to Donald Trump

The Traumatizing Narcissist's Relational System with Daniel Shaw, LCSW

The Heaven's Gate Tragedy—The 20th Anniversary of an American Doomsday Cult Disaster

Jonestown and the Mind Control Cult of Jim Jones: A Survivor's Story

Ministry of Evil: The Twisted Cult of Tony Alamo- A Discussion With Cult Expert and Author Debby Schriver

Keith Raniere and NXIVM on Trial: Mind Control and Manipulation

Former NXIVM Member Sarah Edmondson Talks About Being Recruited Into and Escaping Keith Raniere's Cult

Leaving NXIVM, an Authoritarian Cult, Was Not the End: A Conversation with Sarah Edmondson and Nippy Ames

Unethical Use of Covert Hypnosis to Rape

Videos

Violent Extremism playlist — YouTube

Multi-Level Marketing, Network Marketing exposed - YouTube

Tony Robbins: I Am Not Your Guru - Netflix

The Vow - HBO

Seduced: Inside the NXIVM Cult - Starz

Characteristics of a Cult Leader — Part 1 - YouTube

Characteristics of a Cult Leader — Part 2 - YouTube

Characteristics of a Cult Leader — Part 3 - YouTube

Characteristics of a Cult Leader — Part 4 - YouTube

Characteristics of a Cult Leader — Part 5 - YouTube

Books

On the Edge: Political Cults Right and Left by Dennis Tourish

Examines cult dynamics in political movements, highlighting psychological manipulation, authoritarian tactics, and the parallels with religious cults.

False Profits: Seeking Financial and Spiritual Deliverance in Multi-Level Marketing and Pyramid Schemes by Robert Fitzpatrick and Joyce Reynolds

Critiques MLMs and pyramid schemes, focusing on their exploitative practices, financial and spiritual promises, and the devastating impact on participants.

Traumatic Narcissism: Relational Systems of Subjugation by Daniel Shaw

Explores the concept of traumatic narcissism, detailing how it manifests in relationships and systems, leading to subjugation and psychological harm.

Destroying the World to Save It: Aum Shinrikyo, Apocalyptic Violence, and the New Global Terrorism by Robert Jay Lifton

Analyzes Aum Shinrikyo's apocalyptic ideology and terrorism, offering insights into the psychological and sociopolitical dynamics of cultic violence.

The Guru Papers: Masks of Authoritarian Power Paperback by Joel Kramer and Diana Alstad

Critically examines the authoritarian power dynamics in guru-disciple relationships, revealing the manipulative tactics and psychological control involved.

The Stranger in the Mirror: Dissociation — The Hidden Epidemic by Marlene Steinberg

Discusses dissociation as a widespread yet underrecognized condition, detailing its symptoms, causes, and the journey towards healing.

Whispering in the Daylight: The Children of Tony Alamo Christian Ministries and Their Journey to Freedom by Debby Schriver

Chronicles the experiences of children in Tony Alamo Christian Ministries, highlighting abuse, control, and their paths to recovery.

Let's Sell These People A Piece of Blue Sky by Jon Atack

Offers an in-depth critique of Scientology, focusing on its origins, practices, and the impact on its followers.

Websites

MLM Conference

Pyramid Scheme Alert

Elder Justice

Ending the Game

LaRouche Planet

Multi-Level Marketing Groups Defraud Consumers!

Video discussion in 2014 with Douglas Brooks Esq. and Robert Fitzpatrick, exposing network marketing - YouTube

MODULE 4: INFLUENCE AND CONTROL

Summary: Explores the dynamics of influence and control within cults, including legal and psychological aspects of undue influence.

Learning Objectives: Arm therapists with knowledge on control mechanisms, supporting clients in reclaiming independence and healing from psychological scars.

Module 4 focuses on influence and control. Influence is an inescapable force in everyone's lives, impacting our behaviors and decisions daily. While much of this influence is productive or benign, some is destructive and damaging, leading to a loss of autonomy and individuality. This framework is where the concept of undue influence is essential: a 300-year-old legal term that we can use to describe any act of persuasion that violates our human rights and exploits us psychologically, financially, and even sexually.

This module explores essential aspects of undue influence, how it differs from due influence, and the techniques used to exert it. Additionally, it discusses the use of hypnosis and the ethical considerations that come with it.

We start by revisiting the Influence Continuum, a concept previously introduced in Module 1. Mental health professionals need to comprehend and explain this model to their clients.

Former members need to deconstruct their experiences to help themselves heal. Family members, friends, educators, clergy, and coaches will all benefit by learning to help protect themselves and how to support others. It is one of the most significant models for understanding cult mind control, along with the BITE Model, which addresses Behavior, Information, Thought, and Emotional control.

Dr. Steven Hassan's
BITE MODEL
of Authoritarian Control™

FREEDOM OF MIND®
RESOURCE CENTER

BEHAVIOR CONTROL

1. Regulate individual's physical reality
2. Dictate where, how, and with whom the member lives and associates or isolates
3. When, how and with whom the member has sex
4. Control types of clothing and hairstyles
5. Regulate diet - food and drink, hunger and/or fasting
6. Manipulation and deprivation of sleep
7. Financial exploitation, manipulation or dependence
8. Restrict leisure, entertainment, vacation time
9. Major time spent with group indoctrination and rituals and/or self indoctrination including the Internet
10. Permission required for major decisions
11. Rewards and punishments used to modify behaviors, both positive and negative
12. Discourage individualism, encourage group-think
13. Impose rigid rules and regulations
14. Punish disobedience by beating, torture, burning, cutting, rape, or tattooing/branding
15. Threaten harm to family and friends
16. Force individual to rape or be raped
17. Encourage and engage in corporal punishment
18. Instill dependency and obedience
19. Kidnapping
20. Beating
21. Torture
22. Rape
23. Separation of Families
24. Imprisonment
25. Murder

INFORMATION CONTROL

1. **Deception:**
a. Deliberately withhold information
b. Distort information to make it more acceptable
c. Systematically lie to the cult member

2. **Minimize or discourage access to non-cult sources of information, including:**
a. Internet, TV, radio, books, articles, newspapers, magazines, media
b. Critical information
c. Former members
d. Keep members busy so they don't have time to think and investigate
e. Control through cell phone with texting, calls, internet tracking

3. **Compartmentalize information into Outsider vs. Insider doctrines**
a. Ensure that information is not freely accessible
b. Control information at different levels and missions within group
c. Allow only leadership to decide who needs to know what and when

4. **Encourage spying on other members**
a. Impose a buddy system to monitor and control member
b. Report deviant thoughts, feelings and actions to leadership
c. Ensure that individual behavior is monitored by group

5. **Extensive use of cult-generated information and propaganda, including:**
a. Newsletters, magazines, journals, audiotapes, videotapes, YouTube, movies and other media
b. Misquoting statements or using them out of context from non-cult sources

6. **Unethical use of confession**
a. Information about sins used to disrupt and/or dissolve identity boundaries
b. Withholding forgiveness or absolution
c. Manipulation of memory, possible false memories

THOUGHT CONTROL

1. **Require members to internalize the group's doctrine as truth**
a. Adopting the group's 'map of reality' as reality
b. Instill black and white thinking
c. Decide between good vs. evil
d. Organize people into us vs. them (insiders vs. outsiders)

2. **Change person's name and identity**

3. **Use of loaded language and cliches which constrict knowledge, stop critical thoughts and reduce complexities into platitudinous buzz words**

4. **Encourage only 'good and proper' thoughts**

5. **Hypnotic techniques are used to alter mental states, undermine critical thinking and even to age regress the member**

6. **Memories are manipulated and false memories are created**

7. **Teaching thought-stopping techniques which shut down reality testing by stopping negative thoughts and allowing only positive thoughts, including:**
a. Denial, rationalization, justification, wishful thinking
b. Chanting
c. Meditating
d. Praying
e. Speaking in tongues f. Singing or humming

8. **Rejection of rational analysis, critical thinking, constructive criticism**

9. **Forbid critical questions about leader, doctrine, or policy allowed**

10. **Labeling alternative belief systems as illegitimate, evil, or not useful**

11. **Instill new "map of reality"**

EMOTIONAL CONTROL

1. **Manipulate and narrow the range of feelings – some emotions and/or needs are deemed as evil, wrong or selfish**

2. **Teach emotion-stopping techniques to block feelings of homesickness, anger, doubt**

3. **Make the person feel that problems are always their own fault, never the leader's or the group's fault**

4. **Promote feelings of guilt or unworthiness, such as**
a. Identity guilt
b. You are not living up to your potential
c. Your family is deficient
d. Your past is suspect
e. Your affiliations are unwise
f. Your thoughts, feelings, actions are irrelevant or selfish
g. Social guilt
h. Historical guilt

5. **Instill fear, such as fear of:**
a. Thinking independently
b. The outside world
c. Enemies
d. Losing one's salvation
e. Leaving or being shunned by the group
f. Other's disapproval

6. **Extremes of emotional highs and lows – love bombing and praise one moment and then declaring you are horrible sinner**

7. **Ritualistic and sometimes public confession of sins**

8. **Phobia indoctrination: inculcating irrational fears about leaving the group or questioning the leader's authority**
a. No happiness or fulfillment possible outside of the group
b. Terrible consequences if you leave: hell, demon possession, incurable diseases, accidents, suicide, insanity, 10,000 reincarnations, etc.
c. Shunning of those who leave; fear of being rejected by friends and family
d. Never a legitimate reason to leave; those who leave are weak, undisciplined, unspiritual, worldly, brainwashed by family or counselor, or seduced by money, sex, or rock and roll
e. Threats of harm to ex-member and family

THE INFLUENCE CONTINUUM

The Influence Continuum graphic features three frames to consider: the individual, the leadership, and the organization. Most groups fall somewhere in the middle of the spectrum, leaning towards one end or the other. Most cults I have researched are destructive and authoritarian. Terrorist organizations and criminal groups involved in sex trafficking and slavery are among the most extreme and are often violent. These groups often resort to brutal and violent tactics, including but not limited to rape, torture, imprisonment, and murder.

It's imperative to realize that although cult mentalities may be black-and-white, cults themselves exist on a spectrum, ranging from healthy and constructive, to destructive and unethical. Not all groups with charismatic leaders and devoted followers are dangerous. While some groups resort to deception and restrict information to prevent questioning, others are transparent in recruiting and allow members to read, converse, and depart the group freely.

Everyone can use this framework to differentiate harmless groups from destructive ones. Depending on the criteria, groups may fall at various points along the continuum. I have called my podcast *The Influence Continuum* because I hope to include episodes that share healthy therapeutic methods and not only highlight destructive influence.

INDIVIDUALS

On the healthy side of the continuum, we find empathy, kindness, and love rooted in an individual's intrinsic value. In a healthy setting, the influence acknowledges and celebrates each person's unique qualities, encouraging them to express their authentic selves. Group members can exercise critical thinking and independent decision-making, read, talk, ask questions without restriction, and receive candid and transparent answers. Creativity and humor flourish, providing room for individual expression and community bonding.

In unhealthy groups, love, which is more like praise, is conditional upon obedience and compliance with rules. Destructive cults prioritize ideology over individuality, leading to an "us versus them" mentality and feelings of hatred towards outsiders.

Creativity and humor are limited in these groups and exist only to recruit or maintain membership. A member would be punished if he ever cracked a joke about his messiah or prophet in a way that made that leader look bad. Instead, members are burdened with heavy ideologies that manipulate them emotionally, including love bombing, guilt, and phobia programming.

In destructive groups, the "cult-self" suppresses one's inner voice and conscience, and members must follow orders mindlessly without question. There are no actual permissible free-will choices. If someone exits the cult, they are shunned, derided, and blamed.

At the individual level, there is a significant difference between those born and raised in authoritarian families or cults versus those recruited later in life. The latter tend to have some anchor in the current reality, whereas those born into cults lack exposure to normalcy and a healthy environment.

LEADERS

Healthy leaders are usually psychologically balanced and recognize their limitations. They empower their team members and delegate tasks to those with better skill sets than their own. Healthy leadership is trustworthy and reliable. Ethical leaders honor their commitments and take responsibility for their mistakes, errors, and any harm caused to others.

In contrast, unhealthy leaders are typically malignant narcissists, a personality trait discussed in Module 3. The narcissistic psychopath usually acts out of profound insecurity, while an attachment disorder leads them to compensate for their self-esteem issues. In addition, unhealthy leaders tend to be grandiose and elitist, think they know more than experts in various fields, and are always hungry for power. Moreover, unhealthy leadership tends to be secretive and deceptive, with leaders blaming others and taking no accountability for mistakes or harm caused to others.

ORGANIZATIONS

Healthy organizations operate with checks and balances; they uphold egalitarianism, informed consent, and diversity. Individuals are encouraged to grow and express their unique identities in such groups. Healthy organizations allow people to leave without fear of punishment, threat of shunning, or the creation of phobias.

In contrast, unhealthy organizations exhibit elitism, obedience, dependency, and an authoritarian structure. Such groups promote or demote members based on their compliance with rules, and those who question things may be thrown out or shunned. Unhealthy groups tend to produce clones of the cult leader, in which members begin to adopt their mannerisms and speech patterns, resulting in little room for authentic expression. Destructive groups justify their actions under the guise of "benefiting humanity." They see their goals as so glorious and vital that they believe acts like lying, cheating, and stealing are justified. Moreover, if cult leaders don't actually believe the cult ideology, they still can use it as an excuse to justify actions to their followers.

In unhealthy organizations, there is never a legitimate reason to leave. Those who do leave are labeled as weak, stupid, corrupted by evil entities, or immoral. Leaders of such organizations shift the blame to the individual rather than taking responsibility for their harmful actions and policies.

Unhealthy cults aim to control their victims by isolating them from their families, friends, and other influential individuals. Thus, isolation and control become essential tactics for these groups.

UNDUE INFLUENCE

Influence is an ever-present force in our lives. We are all subject to various social pressures every day in parenting, relationships, media, education, politics, business, religion, and many other facets of daily life. Many types of influence are at work on us all the time, but not everything is undue influence and mind control. Some influence is evident and constructive, such as "Fasten Your Seat Belt" billboards, while other forms of influence are subtle and destructive.

Undue influence traditionally refers to manipulating someone's decisions through coercion or pressure, to turn over one's assets or estate. The BITE Model of Authoritarian Control aims to expand the legal concept—highlighting the sophisticated psychological tactics used by cults and manipulators—to recognize this broader definition in cases of exploitation and abuse.

When I refer to mind control, I specifically address the continuum's destructive end. At its core, mind control promotes dependence and conformity while discouraging autonomy and individuality. It is a system of influence that disrupts an individual's authentic identity and replaces it with a false one.

In most cases, this false identity is something that the person would reject if they had been given informed consent. This is why I also use the term "undue influence." "Undue" because these practices violate personal boundaries, human integrity, ethics, and often the law.

DUE INFLUENCE VS. UNDUE INFLUENCE

Due influence is a positive and ethical form of influence in which individuals or groups use their power, knowledge, and abilities to encourage or persuade others to make informed decisions in their best interest. Due influence involves respecting others' free will and allowing them to make choices that align with their values and beliefs. The focus is building trusting relationships, fostering open communication, and promoting personal growth and development. It seeks to help foster creating positive change for individuals and communities.

In contrast, undue influence, also known as mind control or thought reform, refers to a situation in which a person is manipulated, coerced, or pressured into making a decision or taking an action that is not in their best interest. The person or group exerting undue influence may use deception, flattery, intimidation, hypnosis, or isolation to control the other person's thoughts, behavior, and emotions. Undue influence harms the victim's well-being and autonomy and is on the destructive end of the Influence Continuum.

While the term *undue influence* has mainly been utilized in legal settings, one of my hopes is that the term becomes widely recognized and adopted by the public. In many ways, *undue influence* is more descriptive than *mind control*, as exploitation is part of the definition of undue influence.

The table below outlines the differences between these two types of influence:

Due Influence	Undue Influence
Informed consent	Deception and trickery
Your choice	Manipulation
Right to question	Questioning disallowed
Listening to one's inner voice	Suppressing inner voice
Free to interact with anyone	Isolation and control
Free will	Fear and coercion
Freedom to leave	Enslavement

Psychotherapy should utilize due influence, whereby the therapist works with a client-centered approach to empower them to create positive changes and be their authentic self. Goal-oriented psychotherapy is a practical approach in which the therapist collaborates with the client to set specific targets and achieve them within a predetermined number of sessions. Through due influence, the therapist helps the client to develop their own skills and resources to overcome their challenges and improve their well-being.

Long-term psychotherapy can be problematic since clients may become dependent on the therapist, making it challenging to function autonomously and apply coping strategies and problem-solving skills outside of the therapeutic relationship. Furthermore, the potential for undue influence exists if there aren't concrete therapeutic goals established. Since long-term psychotherapy can create a power dynamic in which the therapist has greater control and influence in the therapeutic relationship, periodic second opinions are often a wise thing to obtain.

ALAN SCHEFLIN'S SOCIAL INFLUENCE MODEL (SIM)

Law professor emeritus Alan Scheflin designed the Social Influence Model (SIM) for expert witnesses to use in the legal system. The model provides a comprehensive framework for evaluating social influence and demonstrates the predator-prey relationship judges and juries must understand to decide whether undue influence exists. In addition to its use in legal contexts, it is also a valuable model for mental health professionals to use to parse out factors such as the Influencer, their identity, and their status in mind control situations.

Here is Scheflin's model:

1. Influencer (Identity and Status) — "Who"

This factor considers the nature of the relationship between the *Influencer* and the *Influencee*, such as whether the Influencer is an authority figure, a confidant, a coach, or a family member. The identity and perceived status of the Influencer play a significant role, as these factors carry weight and power. For instance, does the Influencer hold authority over the Influencee, or are they significantly older or a high-status member of the person's family? In cases of predation, the Influencer or predatory organization often exhibits narcissistic traits such as pathological lying and lack of empathy.

2. Influencer's Motives (Purpose) — "Why"

The motivation of an Influencer may be attributed to financial gain, sexual desires, behavioral compliance, ideological conformity, ego gratification, or political and social power. In the case of cult leaders, they often pursue power, money, and sexual favors from their followers. Unlike con artists who focus solely on monetary gain and move on to their next victim, cult leaders aim to indoctrinate their followers with a new identity that is dependent, pliant, and obedient. Political cult leaders aspire to gain control over local governments, cities, states, countries, or even the world. Meanwhile, sexual predators seek to exert power over their targets, sometimes engaging in a one-time encounter and moving on. In contrast, others seek more prolonged control, like pimps and traffickers who aim to control their targets for monetary gain or to obtain information, as spies might do.

3. Influencer's Methods (Techniques) — "What/How"

The Influencer's Methods refer to the tactics or strategies used to exert control over the Influencee. These methods can range from simple persuasion techniques, such as flattery, to more aggressive tactics, like threats or coercion. Additionally, Influencers may use various forms of manipulation, such as deception, mind games, and gaslighting, to influence their targets. They may also isolate the Influencee from their social support system(s) or use other forms of social pressure to control their behavior. The Influence Continuum and BITE Model offer significant behavioral components to outline the Influencer's methods.

4. Circumstances (Timing & Setting) — "Where/When"

This factor refers to the specific context where social influence occurs, including the time, location, and situation in which the interaction occurs. For example, Influencers may intentionally create certain circumstances that increase their control over the Influencee, such as by using time constraints or creating an environment that induces anxiety or fear. They may also use environmental factors to manipulate the Influencee's perception of reality, such as through lighting or sound effects. Additionally, certain situations may make the Influencee more vulnerable to manipulation, such as when they are experiencing emotional distress or are in a state of heightened suggestibility.

5. Influencee's Receptivity/Vulnerability (Individual Differences) — "Who"

In Module 2, I discussed how individual and situational vulnerabilities could make a person susceptible to cult recruitment. This dynamic aligns with Scheflin's fifth factor, which considers individual differences that may increase a person's susceptibility to social influence. Among these differences are personality traits, emotional states, cognitive abilities, and past experiences. For instance, individuals who are highly suggestible or tend to conform to group norms may be more vulnerable to manipulation by an Influencer. Similarly, individuals who are experiencing emotional distress, who have recently experienced a challenging life event, or who have a history of trauma may be more susceptible to coercion.

6. Consequences (Results) — "What"

The final factor in Alan Scheflin's Social Influence Model is Consequences, which refers to the outcomes or results of social influence, such as the loss of personal autonomy, harm to relationships, or even physical or emotional abuse. The consequences of social influence can be particularly significant in cases of cult recruitment or other forms of coercive control, in which individuals may experience long-lasting psychological harm.

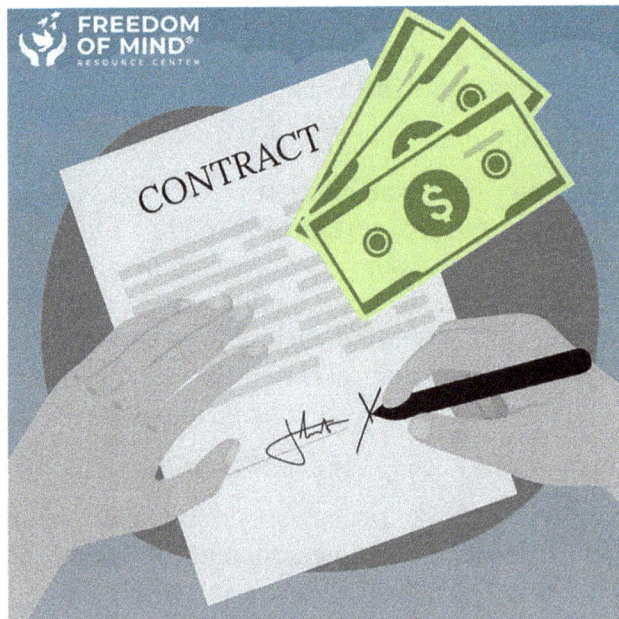

Scheflin's model of social influence highlights how individuals can be manipulated into agreements through pressure, trust, and authority, without informed consent and capacity to understand the consequences of their actions.

Scheflin's Social Influence Model provides a comprehensive framework for evaluating social influence and coercion. Mental health professionals can use the model to understand the dynamics of undue influence better and to help former cult members address the specific harms they have experienced, regain their sense of autonomy, and work towards healing and recovery.

This model was a significant feature of my doctoral dissertation, _The BITE Model of Authoritarian Control: Undue Influence, Thought Reform, Brainwashing, Mind Control, Trafficking, and the Law._ I talk about Scheflin's Social Influence Model at the beginning of Module 8 in the course. Still, I decided to include information about it here since it is relevant to the discussion of undue influence.

Scheflin's Social Influence Model (SIM) was inspired by Rudyard Kipling's poem, _I Keep Six Honest Serving Men._ The six men Kipling names in this poem are What, Why, When, How, Where, and Who. Scheflin realized that these six "men" are the essential elements of all storytelling and would be very useful to describe the contours of the undue influence theory.

I think it is vital for you to understand this model. In some cases, you may wish to give homework to your client to read the blogs on freedomofmind.com on SIM and then discuss with them how they think it applies to their experience in a cult or undue influence situation. A client might not be aware that the influencer had bad intentions. I think encouraging research, sometimes with a Private Investigator (PI), if necessary (Google can often turn up things as well as webarchive.org), is a good investment. These sites might be able to help you find past lawsuits and criminal behavior in the influencer's past. Perhaps the influencers had been in a destructive cult themselves. Or an abusive authoritarian family. Perhaps the P.I. can locate other victims.

Another reason this framework is powerful in helping people heal is that many of my clients have been taught to believe that "there is no such thing as a victim." Under this view, they have been programmed to believe that everything bad that has happened was their creation, their choice.

I argue that this is a toxic belief and serves abusers. It also can create a blaming and shaming framework. This dynamic would often lead to the person believing they somehow created the rape or mugging, for example. This belief is flat-out wrong. We are not "God," and we don't create reality. Bad things happen to good people. Coincidences happen. Humans often like to link causality to occurrences when there are none.

REFLECTIVE EXERCISES

1. How can the Social Influence Model help therapists better understand clients' experiences who have suffered undue influence?

_____

_____

_____

_____

_____

_____

_____

_____

_____

_____

_____

_____

SUBTLE VS. EXTREME UNDUE INFLUENCE

Undue influence can manifest in both subtle and extreme forms. Subtle forms of undue influence occur when the "agent of influence"—such as a partner, friend, teacher, or employer—is perceived as benevolent or neutral. Victims may believe they entered a relationship or group of their own free will, but were actually deceptively recruited or manipulated. Gaslighting can and does occur in relationships with an intimate partner. As time passes, the victim's authentic self is replaced with a new identity that adheres to a different belief system and behavior code, which they may believe is a result of their choice rather than manipulation. I have worked with many people who said they were just having "fun" and decided to see a psychic and get a "reading." Some people I have worked with were getting high and watching YouTube videos late into the night. No one told them to watch; instead, AI algorithms influenced them based on their online profile. Dopamine addiction can keep people rapt for long periods on social media platforms.

In the most extreme forms of undue influence, the agent of influence is perceived as malevolent right from the outset. For example, victims may be subjected to drugging, kidnapping, imprisonment, torture, or coercion through force. The outcome is compliance and trauma bonding, which forms a new identity in the cult member that is both obedient and dependent.

A striking example of this is the case of Patty Hearst, who was abducted at gunpoint by a political cult, the Symbionese Liberation Army (SLA). The cult kidnapped her and subjected her to rape, abuse, and indoctrination. Eventually, she became a trusted cult member named "Tania." She was arrested for her involvement in a bank robbery and at a sporting goods store. After she exited the cult and got counseling, her sentence was commuted.

MIND CONTROL VS. BRAINWASHING

In widespread discussion, *brainwashing* is often used synonymously with *mind control*. However, I used to think of brainwashing as more damaging and destructive. Mind control is a form of subtle undue influence, as defined in the section above, while brainwashing is extreme.

The table below outlines the differences between these two terms:

Mind Control	Brainwashing
Voluntary participation and cooperation	Physical imprisonment, torture, or overt coercion
In the beginning, mind controllers are viewed as friends or benign	In the beginning, brainwashers are regarded as the enemy
Produces new identity and internalization of new beliefs	Produces compliant behavior (e.g., false confessions)

The term "brainwashing" was first coined by journalist and CIA agent Edward Hunter in 1951 to describe how American servicemen captured during the Korean War suddenly changed their values and allegiances and came to believe they had committed fictitious war crimes. Hunter derived the term from the Chinese phrase "*hsi nao*," which translates to "wash brain." However, the term brainwashing is inaccurate, as the mind cannot be compared to a blackboard that can be wiped clean and rewritten with new content.

I used to think of brainwashing as an overtly coercive technique, in which the victim is aware from the start that they are in the hands of an adversary. The process begins with clearly delineating roles, with the prisoner or victim having minimal agency. Physical abuse, torture, and even sexual assault may be employed.

Brainwashing is especially effective in producing compliance with demands, such as signing a false confession or denouncing one's government. Individuals may comply out of a need for self-preservation; over time, their beliefs may shift to justify their actions. However, these beliefs are often not deeply ingrained. When individuals are no longer under the influence and fear of their captors, they often discard these beliefs.

Unlike brainwashing, mind control is a much more subtle and sophisticated technique. The victim often perceives the controllers as peers or friends, making them less guarded and more willing to cooperate. The individual may unwittingly divulge personal information that will be used against them. Mind control utilizes hypnotic processes and group dynamics to create a potent indoctrination effect without relying on overt physical abuse. The victim is deceived and manipulated into making the desired choices without direct threats. Although the victim may initially respond positively, the outcome is ultimately harmful and destructive.

I have found myself deciding to use the term brainwashing much more loosely, especially in recent years since Trump became President of the U.S. in 2016. This has largely been to serve public understanding surrounding the colloquial usage of the term. When helping someone recover, pay attention to your client's reactions to words. Some of my clients have insisted I use the term brainwashing. Others have resisted its use. Undue influence is more acceptable for many.

BENIGN CULTS VS. HARMFUL CULTS

The term "cult" is problematic for many people (including scholars) because it is imprecise and subjective, meaning different things to different people. In the context of groups, it is typically used only negatively, implying that the group is dangerous, abusive, or extremist. However, there are also benign, harmless, positive cults around physical fitness, self-improvement, or healthy spiritual practices.

Benign cult groups are made of people who follow a set of beliefs and rituals. If people can join the group freely with informed consent, including full and honest disclosure of the group's doctrine and practices, and can choose to leave without shunning, fear, or harassment, then it is most likely not a destructive cult. This category may include fans of a sports team, musician, or popular game. For example, Bruce Springsteen has a devoted fan base who call him the Boss. Still, they are free to leave a concert, express dislike of a song or album, and appreciate other musicians without fear of repercussions. People laugh when I tell them that I was included in the book *The Cult of Mac* as someone who learned computers in the early 1980s on Apple products and has never bought a PC or Android device.

For most of my work, when I use the term "cult," I am talking about destructive cults, not healthy, benign, or productive cults. As therapists, we must also be cautious when using the word "cult" with our clients, as it can be a roadblock to lucidity, marring the possibility of candid discussion. Even if the client uses the term themselves, it is essential to ask them to clarify what they mean and help them own the word's negative application. If they prefer not to use the term, you can refer to their group as a movement, organization, or group to avoid negative associations that could interfere with the therapeutic process.

REFLECTIVE EXERCISES

2. Think of a time when you felt influenced by a person or group positively. What made this influence positive? How did it benefit you?

_____
_____
_____
_____
_____
_____
_____
_____
_____
_____
_____
_____
_____
_____
_____
_____

3. Consider a situation in which you were pressured to decide or take an action not aligned with your values or beliefs. What methods were used to pressure you or influence your decision? How did you feel during and after this experience?

_____

_____

_____

_____

_____

_____

_____

_____

_____

_____

_____

_____

4. Imagine a client who has been subjected to undue influence. How could you use healthy influence to empower them to create positive changes and be their authentic self?

_____

_____

_____

_____

_____

_____

_____

_____

_____

_____

_____

_____

CASE STUDY: PATRICIA HEARST

One of the most famous cases of brainwashing and cult mind control in the United States involved <u>Patty Hearst</u>. In 1974, Patricia Hearst, the 19-year-old granddaughter of media mogul William Hearst, was kidnapped from her Berkeley, California apartment by a left-wing extremist group known as the Symbionese Liberation Army (SLA). The SLA was a small, radical terrorist cult based in America committed to overthrowing the U.S. government and establishing a new, socialist society.

For the next two months, the SLA held her captive in a closet-sized room, subjected her to physical and psychological abuse, food deprivation, rape, and exposure to a barrage of political propaganda. Finally, the SLA demanded that the Hearst family pay a ransom of $70 million and distribute free food to people experiencing poverty in exchange for Patty's release.

On April 15, 1974, Patty appeared on surveillance footage robbing a bank in San Francisco with members of the SLA. Patty had taken on a new identity, "Tania," and had reportedly joined the SLA. Over the next several months, Patty passed up chances to escape and was involved in a series of violent crimes, including a shoot-out with police.

When Patty was finally captured in September 1975, she was charged with armed robbery. Patty's defense team decided to argue that the SLA manipulated her into joining their cause and participating in their crimes. At the final summation, her attorney, F. Lee Bailey, abandoned that approach. The jurors ultimately rejected the idea of brainwashing and convicted Patty of armed robbery. The prosecution had argued that Patty had willingly joined the SLA and had participated in their crimes of her own free will. They argued that the SLA had not used brainwashing techniques but had persuaded Patty to join their cause through ideology and group dynamics. There were claims that Patty and the cult member who raped her had a consensual love affair. No doubt there was trauma bonding.

Patty was sentenced to 35 years in prison, later reduced to 7 years. President Jimmy Carter commuted her sentence, and President Bill Clinton pardoned her in 2001.

REFLECTIVE EXERCISES

5. What techniques did the SLA use to brainwash Patty Hearst?

_____

_____

_____

_____

_____

_____

_____

_____

_____

_____

6. Based on the information in this module, what factors should have been considered during Patty Hearst's trial?

_____

_____

_____

_____

_____

_____

_____

_____

_____

7. In what ways can the case of Patty Hearst influence your therapeutic approach when working with clients who have been subjected to undue influence and may be experiencing guilt over any wrongful actions they may have taken during that time?

_____

_____

_____

_____

_____

_____

_____

_____

_____

_____

_____

HOW DOES UNDUE INFLUENCE HAPPEN?

As Module 2 highlights, undue influence can impact anyone. The commonly held notion that only weak or vulnerable individuals can be recruited into cults is a misconception that allows people to distance themselves from the frightening possibility of falling prey to cult recruitment. This false sense of invulnerability to undue influence overlooks the reality that we are all susceptible to mind control.

Deceptive recruitment tactics can lure anyone, especially during situational vulnerability, such as losing a loved one or ending a relationship. The ongoing pandemic has also left people increasingly vulnerable to online recruitment and indoctrination due to prolonged social isolation and financial struggles.

Additionally, various individual vulnerabilities, such as learning and developmental disabilities, addictions, or early childhood trauma, can make one susceptible to undue influence. However, the most significant vulnerability is a lack of education about the techniques used in cult mind control.

Undue influence can also happen through hypnotic processes, which can induce a trance-like state where an individual is more suggestible and open to manipulation. Hypnosis can be used in subtle and extreme forms of undue influence and is often combined with other tactics, such as isolation and control, to create a potent indoctrination effect.

HYPNOSIS

Hypnosis is an often misunderstood phenomenon. People who undergo hypnosis enter a trance-like state fundamentally different from ordinary consciousness. The critical difference is that, in normal consciousness, one's attention is focused outwards through the five senses, while in a trance-like state, one's attention is usually focused inwards. This range of difference can range from mild trance states, such as daydreaming, to deeper states in which one is less aware of the outside world and highly susceptible to suggestion.

Under a hypnosis framework, it is valuable to understand that humans primarily experience life through five primary senses: visual, auditory, kinesthetic (physical sensations), olfactory (smell), and gustatory (taste). Our brains have circuitry for these inputs, and likewise, we store memories with information taken in during experiences, even when we aren't consciously aware. The latest science says that the brain can and does take in approximately eleven million bits of information a second, while our conscious minds can only process forty-fifty bits of information a second. Therefore, we can be influenced a great deal — especially when we are in an environment with other people — without realizing it. We know people can adapt quickly to new environments, which is potentially a strength. However, it can also be a liability when it comes to destructively controlling groups and people.

One hypnotic phenomenon particularly worth explaining in the context of cults is hallucination. In the world of hypnosis, people can experience both positive and negative hallucinations, sometimes mistakenly interpreted as good and bad hallucinations. Positive hallucinations occur when someone perceives something that isn't there, such as imagining seeing a rose or experiencing a rose's smell. The person may be remembering a past experience, projecting their imagination, or a bit of both. However, they experience it as being real, even when it is not.

Negative hallucination is the mental process of erasing awareness of something that is real and present, causing it to disappear from conscious perception. This phenomenon can include the ability to make television cameras disappear when participating in an interview or blocking out hecklers when playing a sport.

These techniques can also be used to install false memories of experiences that never happened. They can also be used to induce confabulation of extrapolated events from a distant memory of something that did happen. In the programming of my Moonie identity, the group used a single incident when my father slapped my cheek when I lied to him to create a strong belief that I had been abused as a child and had a miserable childhood.

When used by experienced, credentialed professionals, hypnosis can serve as a robust set of tools that can help people tremendously. It can improve emotional well-being, concentration, sleep, and immune system function, altogether promoting healthy behaviors.

In addition, when used therapeutically by a mental health expert, <u>hypnosis can facilitate recovery from trauma</u>. Ultimately, <u>ethical hypnosis</u> empowers people to tap into their potential and achieve optimal functioning.

Regrettably, anything that possesses the ability to heal also has the potential to cause harm, and hypnosis is not an exception. Many people are exposed to hypnosis by entertainers on stage or in YouTube videos with no credentials or appropriate training. The majority of these "shows" or videos are highly problematic. People are made to believe they are chickens, clucking and walking like one on stage while the audience laughs at them. While this use of hypnosis is mostly harmless, it induces an altered state of consciousness in which the individual's critical thinking faculties are temporarily suppressed, rendering them highly susceptible to suggestion.

Imagination is a powerful tool, and an adept hypnotist can achieve incredible outcomes with it, particularly with highly hypnotizable individuals. Nonetheless, far more concerning things being propagated online are unethical, dangerous, and criminal. Some individuals are learning to <u>covertly hypnotize others to rape them</u> or are being exposed to videos encouraging them to believe they are of the opposite sex.

MY PATHWAY INTO HYPNOSIS

When I was in the Moon cult, I was instructed to model our leaders' behavior. I was told to be a small Sun Myung Moon and think like him, feel like him, and behave as he would. I was also told to engage in extensive prayer and observe my superiors to replicate their actions. In doing so, I acquired hypnotic techniques for recruiting new members. I thought I was "growing spiritually," but in reality I was undergoing a process of becoming a clone of Sun Myung Moon. At the time, I was unaware of these techniques and simply identified and mimicked the behaviors modeled to me.

Four years after leaving the Moonies cult (in May 1976), in 1980, I attended a seminar by hypnotist Richard Bandler. Bandler was a co-founder of Neuro-Linguistic Programming (NLP) with John Grinder. During that workshop, I realized that the missing ingredient to my research in social psychology was the hypnotic manipulation of people's states of consciousness. The seminar gave me insight into techniques of hypnotic mind control. It was the "missing link" that filled in so much about influence. So, I decided to learn everything I could.

I spent nearly two years studying NLP, becoming trained as both a practitioner and a master practitioner. I even relocated to Santa Cruz, California, to pursue an apprenticeship with John Grinder. I learned from all of the early teachers of NLP as I learned to become a trainer. However, as time passed, my concerns over the ethical implications of NLP grew. Its leaders had shifted their focus towards promoting NLP as a tool for power enhancement, launching a mass-market campaign to train salespeople and business executives. This shift departed from their original emphasis on training therapists and educators.

One of my main issues with NLP was their motto of "Do what works," which I believed to be amoral. While licensed therapists adhere to strict ethical guidelines, the same could not be guaranteed for corporate executives seeking power, money, or sex. Consequently, I decided to end my affiliation with NLP permanently.

In 1985, I obtained my master's degree in counseling psychology from Cambridge College, which allowed me to receive training from some of the top ethical practitioners in clinical hypnosis. This education equipped me with a better understanding of applying my knowledge to help individuals trapped in cults. I realized that it was possible to develop a model encompassing the entire change process that occurs when a person is drawn into a cult and then successfully exits it. It's important to note that I generally refrain from using clinical hypnosis with clients who have undergone cult or undue influence unless in exceptional circumstances. Instead, I focus on educating my clients about hypnosis and assisting them in identifying how it was used in their cult programming.

HYPNOSIS IN MIND CONTROL CULTS

Cults use hypnosis to exert unhealthy influence or mind control over members. In many religious or spiritual cults, what is often called "meditation" is really a process by which the cult members are induced to enter a trance. During this time, they may receive suggestions that make them more receptive to following the cult's doctrine. Non-religious cults use other forms of group or individual induction.

Cult leaders often use hypnosis as a means of instilling phobias and coercing people into thinking that terrible things will happen to them if they ever decide to leave the cult. In addition, they may have used hypnotic processes to convince people to harm themselves and others. Members are typically unaware that they are being hypnotized or put into a highly suggestible state. For example, Hubbard, the creator of the Scientology cult, was a hypnotist, and the Training Routines were intended to create trance states.

A few years ago, I met with Mike Rinder, former head of Scientology's Office of Special Affairs (OSA). Mike was a member of Scientology for over 46 years. I sat with Mike and his wife the day after he and Leah Remini were honored at a ChildUSA.org fundraiser and explained that Scientology used hypnotic techniques. He was resistant to the very idea as a lingering effect of his indoctrination. At the time, he maintained a skeptical stance.

In Scientology, in one of the beginner Training Routines (TRs), participants are told to sit and stare blankly with their feet flat on the floor as they are yelled at and insulted.

Destructive cults frequently induce trances in their members through prolonged indoctrination sessions. Techniques such as repetition, monotony, and enforced attentiveness are conducive to inducing a trance. When observing a group in such a setting, it becomes apparent to a trained outsider when the trance has taken hold. The audience's blink-and-swallow reflexes slow down, and their facial expressions relax into a blank, neutral state. When people are in this state, it becomes possible for unethical leaders to implant irrational beliefs. I find it very important to teach my clients about hypnosis and help them understand and apply this knowledge as they unpack their experiences.

In some cases, I show videos of the U.K. entertainer Derren Brown. Or I might show a TED talk video with a stage hypnotist demonstration. Sometimes, I share audio or videotapes of other cult leaders, like Yogi Bhajan or Rajneesh (Osho), speaking hypnotically.

Some of the hypnotic processes adopted by unhealthy leaders and groups include the following:

- *Mirroring:* This is a Neuro-Linguistic Programming (NLP) technique that entails behaviorally mimicking an individual's voice patterns, tonality, speech, speed, posture, and/or breathing patterns. Cult recruiters frequently employ this technique, often unconsciously, sometimes intentionally (such as in the case they have been trained to use NLP). Mirroring creates a sense of familiarity or trust with the recruiter, who is essentially mimicking them. Many people report experiencing the stranger as someone they have known their whole life. And, indeed, they have, because that person is themselves!

- *Mystical manipulation:* This practice typically entails fabricating a spiritual illusion when, in reality, it is nothing more than a trick. In other instances, information may be surreptitiously collected about a person. The cult leader or recruiter may subsequently divulge this information to the person, attributing it to God or their purported psychic abilities. Mystical manipulation is one of Robert Jay Lifton's eight criteria of thought reform.

- *Magic tricks:* Some cult leaders use magic tricks to convince their followers that they possess special powers or abilities. For instance, Sai Baba proclaimed himself to be a reincarnation of a famous mystic and would allegedly materialize Rolex watches out of nothing, attributing this sleight of hand to his supposed spiritual powers. Similarly, debunked clairvoyant and faith healer Peter Popoff would feign knowledge about audience members when he was actually receiving information through a hearing device called the magician's ear from one of his people.

- *Memory manipulation:* Hypnosis can be used to manipulate memories, including confabulation of existing memories and implantation of false ones. This may include the creation of memories of physical, sexual, or emotional abuse that never occurred.

PROTECTING YOURSELF AND OTHERS FROM UNETHICAL HYPNOSIS

It is crucial to protect yourself and your clients from unethical hypnosis and learn how to mitigate its adverse effects.

- *Professional accountability:* I advise individuals considering hypnotherapy to seek a qualified hypnotherapist who holds appropriate credentials and is affiliated with professional organizations. I am a member of the American Society of Clinical Hypnosis and the International Society for Hypnosis, both of which provide guidance for finding accredited practitioners.
  Many stage hypnotists and others take a short course and start hypnotizing people. Beware of these folks. Some offer certificates and credentials, but I don't recommend these programs or NLP practitioners who aren't licensed mental health professionals.

- *Retriggering previous experiences:* Improper hypnotherapy techniques can retrigger past traumas and experiences. For example, simply hearing discussions about hypnosis can induce a trance-like state in former cult members, resulting in dilated pupils, relaxed muscle tone, and altered affect. Therapists can assist individuals by employing grounding techniques to help them remain present in the moment.

- *Psychoeducation and informed consent:* As you have learned, I believe therapists must provide psychoeducation to former cult members about how hypnosis can be used to manipulate and deceive and how these techniques may have been used to recruit them into the cult. In addition, if you are a mental health practitioner, pursue training with ASCH.org before you attempt to use this powerful modality with folks who have been unduly influenced. Make sure they are fully informed about the process and the potential risks and benefits. Ensure they provide their consent for each aspect of the treatment. To ensure safety and transparency, if you seek therapy with a hypnotherapist, ensure they have taken this course and are familiar with the cult you were involved in. I advise against going into trance states with people you don't know well and haven't checked out as having credibility and integrity. An ethical hypnotherapist will permit the recording of the entire session.

- *Differences between experiences and facts:* Therapists need to educate their clients and offer support and validation of their growth process. This education should include strategies, techniques, and models to help clients distinguish between factual events and experiences that may have been generated through hypnosis. Clients may have experienced things they perceive as impossible or mystical and will need to be supported and educated through deconstructing these experiences.

- *Incremental compliance*: Incremental compliance in cults refers to gradually increasing an individual's involvement in the group through small requests or demands that are initially easy to comply with, but become increasingly difficult or extreme over time. The ultimate goal of incremental compliance is to make the individual more vulnerable to the group's influence and to increase their commitment to the group's ideology and practices. Incremental compliance in hypnosis is when the hypnotist gradually increases the complexity and intensity of suggestions so that they will adopt new beliefs or behaviors.

- *Caution and consent:* A cornerstone of my model of working with people who have been victims of undue influence is to empower them to take control of their thoughts and beliefs, develop an internal locus of control for their lives, and be anchored in their authentic selves. This process involves helping them to live in the present with a positive future outlook and teaching them how to discern between healthy and unhealthy people and groups. Given the potential risks associated with hypnosis, it must always be used cautiously and with the individual's informed consent.

REFLECTIVE EXERCISES

8. Have you ever undergone hypnosis? If so, was it a positive or negative experience? In what ways? If you have not, what do you think it would be like? How would you know you were hypnotized?

_____

_____

_____

_____

_____

_____

_____

_____

_____

_____

_____

9. How might therapists educate and support clients who have experienced mind control involving hypnotic techniques?

_____

_____

_____

_____

_____

_____

_____

_____

_____

_____

_____

_____

DSM-V-TR CLASSIFICATION

In Module 1, I discussed the DSM-V-TR classification that acknowledges the psychological effects of mind control, and I want to emphasize its importance again in this module. It can be a grounding and validating experience for clients to understand that their experiences are recognized as legitimate and that the issues they are facing are real. Below is a description of this disorder from the DSM-V-TR.

DSM-V-TR: Other Specified Dissociative Disorder (F44.89)

Identity disturbance due to prolonged and intense coercive persuasion: Individuals who have been subjected to intense coercive persuasion (e.g., brainwashing, thought reform, indoctrination while captive, torture, long-term political imprisonment, recruitment by sects/cults or by terror organizations) may present with prolonged changes in, or conscious questioning of, their identity.

Many therapists and practitioners are unaware that a diagnosis of mind control can be made, supported by the DSM-5-TR, and may not be familiar with specialized treatment approaches developed to address it. As a result, individuals affected by cult involvement may continue to suffer without receiving the help they need. Still, a few individuals have recognized this population's unique needs and are willing and able to provide specialized treatment to help them recover. I hope this course will contribute to this process and help raise awareness of this population's unique challenges.

Undue influence is a pervasive and destructive force in our society. It is a system of influence that aims to replace an individual's authentic identity with a false one through deception. While some influence is benign and helpful, undue influence violates personal boundaries, human integrity, ethics, and even the law. Therefore, we must understand the differences between due and undue influence and the various techniques used to implement them. By being informed and vigilant, we can protect ourselves and our loved ones from falling prey to undue influence and mind control.

MODULE 4 RESOURCES

Freedom of Mind Resources

Important New Model Offers Legal Guidelines for Cases Involving Undue Influence

The Anatomy of Undue Influence: Scientific Study and Elsevier Journal Article

Evaluating Undue Influence in Legal & Mental Health Settings

Evaluating Undue Influence: Scheflin's Model as a Framework

Scheflin — Hassan Talk on Legal Issues of Brainwashing and Undue Influence

Evaluating Undue Influence: Scheflin's Model as a Framework

Professor Alan Scheflin's Social Influence Model (SIM)

The Radicalization of Patty Hearst: Mind Control by the SLA, a Political Cult

New Book on Patty Hearst Falls Short of Understanding Undue Influence

Unethical Use of Covert Hypnosis to Rape

A Paradigm Shift for Health: A Biopsychosocial Model of Hypnosis

The Therapeutic Use of Hypnosis to Improve Health and Recover From Trauma with Laurence Sugarman MD

Hypnosis, Guided Meditation, Deep Visualizations—Consumers Beware!

Videos

Spotting a Cult, Hidden Hypnotism & Indoctrination in the Digital Age

The Radicalization of Patty Hearst: Mind Control by the SLA, a Political Cult

Hypnosis, Guided Meditation, Deep Visualizations—Consumers Beware!

Books

The Rape of the Mind: The Psychology of Thought Control, Menticide, and Brainwashing by Joost A.M. Meerloo

This book delves into thought control, menticide, and brainwashing techniques used by totalitarian regimes to suppress individuality and enforce conformity, emphasizing psychological resilience as a defense.

Changing Minds with Clinical Hypnosis by Lee Warner Brooks, Laurence Sugarman, and Julie Linden

This book offers a comprehensive guide on using hypnosis in therapy, detailing its theoretical foundations, practical applications, and potential for facilitating significant psychological change and healing.

MODULE 5: THEORIES AND MODELS OF MIND CONTROL

Summary: Offers an in-depth look at various theories and models related to mind control, facilitating a deeper understanding of cult influence.

Learning Objectives: Enhance therapists' conceptualization of clients' experiences within cults, leading to targeted and effective therapeutic interventions.

In this module, we delve into some of the critical models that have been instrumental in highlighting the tactics used by authoritarian groups to gain control over their members. One model is social psychologist Leon Festinger's Cognitive Dissonance Theory. Another model is the Chinese Communist brainwashing programs of the 1950s. These include psychiatrist Robert Jay Lifton's Thought Reform Model, which cites eight criteria. Psychologist Margaret Singer created a model called 6 Conditions for Thought Reform.

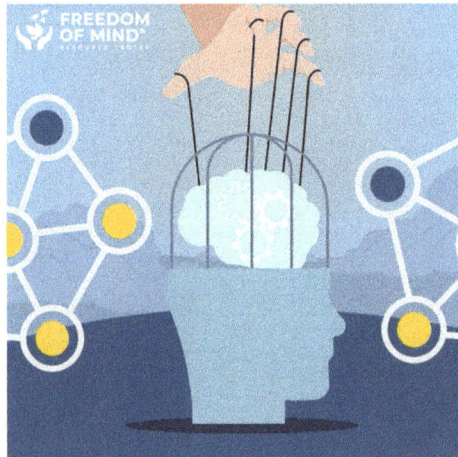

Understanding various models of undue influence and thought reform equips clinicians with essential tools to identify and address the psychological tactics used by authoritarian groups.

My <u>BITE Model of Authoritarian Control</u> (as already mentioned) is my contribution to these models, utilizing and incorporating the above-mentioned models.

Understanding these models as a clinician is valuable in recognizing strategies destructive cults use to control their followers and helps protect individuals from falling prey to such undue influence. By understanding them, you can incorporate these important principles as part of client psychoeducation.

Over the years, many different terms have been used to describe mind control, including brainwashing, thought reform, psychological manipulation, menticide, coercive persuasion, and unethical hypnosis.

Additional terms like undue influence, coercive control, predatory alienation, psychological programming, psychological torture, trafficking, and slavery have all been used to describe a leader's or group's exploitative influence over an individual. While all of these terms capture the damaging impact of such influence, <u>undue influence</u> is the most widely recognized term within the legal system. Indeed, coercive control is illegal in the U.K. However, as of this moment, its focus is only on domestic abuse cases. This term is gaining legal recognition in some countries, including the United States. Familiarity with these terms is essential in identifying and combating the tactics used by authoritarian groups to manipulate and harm individuals.

COGNITIVE DISSONANCE THEORY
SOCIAL PSYCHOLOGIST LEON FESTINGER

Leon Festinger was a student of the famous social psychologist Kurt Lewin. Festinger developed the theory of cognitive dissonance in the 1950s after studying the effects of cognitive inconsistency.

Festinger, who co-authored the book *When Prophecy Fails*, studied a UFO apocalyptic cult. He and his students were curious about why people did not lose faith and leave the cult group when the spacecraft failed to appear on the designated mountain at the prophesized time.

Counterintuitively, many believers became even more firmly committed to their belief in aliens. Festinger proposed that humans dislike psychological conflict and prefer consistency to align their thoughts, feelings, and behaviors.

People are motivated to resolve the inconsistency in a way that restores cognitive harmony, which they do in various ways, including changing their attitudes or behaviors, seeking out information that supports their beliefs, or minimizing the importance of the inconsistency. This concept laid the foundation for all cognitive-behavioral therapy.

When a person's behavior changes, their thoughts and feelings will change to minimize dissonance. Moreover, this principle is interchangeable: altering a person's beliefs can lead to changes in their emotions and behaviors, or modifying their feelings can lead to changes in their beliefs and behaviors.

My BITE Model was developed by understanding how thoughts, feelings, and behaviors influence each other. The BITE Model was explicated in writing first in my 1985 Master's project. At that time, I could not conceive of future technological developments like the Internet, smartphones, social media, and Artificial Intelligence (AI).

REFLECTIVE EXERCISES

1. What strategies can therapists use to help clients identify and challenge any remaining beliefs or behaviors from their cult experience that are inconsistent with their new values and goals after leaving a cult?

_____

_____

_____

_____

_____

_____

_____

_____

_____

_____

ROBERT JAY LIFTON'S THOUGHT REFORM MODEL

Psychiatrist Robert Jay Lifton's seminal work _Thought Reform and the Psychology of Totalism: A Study of "Brainwashing" in China_ was published in 1961. Chapter 22 of his book, titled "Ideological Totalism," outlines eight criteria that must be present in a thought reform environment. Lifton acknowledges that some of these criteria are also present in groups considered "normal," including his experience in medical school. Lifton's understanding of these criteria is based on interviews he conducted with individuals who had experienced Chinese thought reform during the 1950s. Lifton cites these eight criteria in his later books *Destroying the World to Save It* and *Losing Reality*.

I was first introduced to Lifton's book during my deprogramming in May 1976. It helped me understand that the tactics used by the Moonies to indoctrinate me were similar to those used by Mao's Communist China. After my recovery, I reached out to Lifton while he was teaching at Yale University and met with him. When I explained the Moonie indoctrination process to him, he said that what I described was like a virulent mutation of what he had studied. He also said that while I had lived through it, he had only learned it second-hand. He encouraged me to study psychology and share my knowledge with others. His words gave me a new purpose and ultimately led me to become a licensed mental health counselor, author, and educator.

Lifton's "Eight Criteria of Thought Reform," which he later referred to as "The Eight Deadly Sins," have proven helpful in identifying many situations involving undue influence. These criteria include milieu control, mystical manipulation, demand for purity, cult of confession, sacred science, loaded language, doctrine over person, and dispensing of existence.

1. MILIEU CONTROL

This criterion is about control of the environment and communication within that environment. This includes what people communicate with each other and how the group gets inside a person's head and controls their internal dialogue. Removing a recruit from the totalistic environment and lifting the milieu control allows the individual's authentic self to reemerge. There can be a sudden lifting of the cult identity when a person who has been in a cult is abruptly exposed to outside, alternative influences.

2. MYSTICAL MANIPULATION

With mystical manipulation, there is the contrived engineering of experiences to stage seemingly spontaneous and supernatural events. Cult members wrongly attribute divine forces to what is trickery. They may believe that the leader is reading their mind or that there are magical forces at work to explain why things happened the way they did. Leaders are often seen as "mediators for God." This "chosen" human being is viewed as a savior or a source of salvation.

One example is when a person is invited to a cult "Bible study" without realizing that the recruiter was instructed to learn about his background and report it to the leader. So, when the Bible study is conducted, key teachings would be used to give the new person the subjective feeling that God knew all about him and his struggles and was directing him to become involved.

3. DEMAND FOR PURITY

Demand for purity is establishing impossible standards for performance. In this case, no matter how hard a person tries, he always falls short, feels terrible, and works even harder. Demand for purity can also include "perfectionism" and the internalization of the incorrect belief that human beings can be perfect. The demand for purity can create a Manichean quality in cults, as in other religious and political groups. Such a demand for purity calls for separating pure and impure, good and evil, within an environment and oneself. This process creates an atmosphere of guilt and shame, which can be used and manipulated emotionally.

4. THE CULT OF CONFESSION

The cult of confession entails the destruction of personal boundaries and the expectation that every thought, feeling, or action, past or present, that does not align with the group's rules be shared or confessed. This information is not forgotten or forgiven but used to control the individual. The cult or leader uses their knowledge about an individual to make them conform and obey. If the individual does not respond as expected, they are shamed. The cult or controller believes they have the right to know everything about the individual's life. The individual has no right to keep any secrets, including negative thoughts and feelings about the controller. Within the confession process, thought reform is conducted with a structured pattern of criticism and self-criticism during sessions where individuals confess their sins. These sessions typically occur within small groups and have an active thrust toward personal change.

5. SACRED SCIENCE

Sacred science refers to the firm conviction that the teachings and doctrines of the group are the only scientifically and morally objective truths, with no scope for questioning or opposing perspectives. At this elevated level, the group's principles must be perceived as the highest moral authority. Sacred science can provide significant assurance to young individuals as it simplifies the world's complexities.

The Moon cult utilized scholarly conferences that even Nobel Laureates attended, creating an air of legitimacy in their espoused mission to "unify science and religion" and bring about world change. Today, the digital landscape is filled with numerous conspiracy theory cults that claim scientific legitimacy while promoting grand ideas without scientific evidence.

Individuals deeply entrenched in cult ideologies often lack an understanding of the nature of science, which is a constantly evolving process that relies on community collaboration. Rather than being a static ideology, science involves the testing and refining hypotheses through scrutiny, challenge, and replication of evidence. True believers in cult ideologies fail to recognize that theories are merely beliefs subject to scientific validation and may be abandoned or modified when new evidence emerges.

6. LOADING THE LANGUAGE

In contrast to healthy application of an extensive vocabulary for navigating the world, an individual under mind control is restricted to a significantly limited set of words and concepts exclusive to the cult. This constriction and compression of language limit the capacity to contemplate reality's subtleties, intricacies, and complexities.

Loading the language involves the process of literalizing language, in which words or images become sacred or divine. Cults use a specific set of coded symbols, expressions, buzzwords, clichés, and platitudes unique to their group to foster group coherence. This "cult speak" can have significant appeal and psychological power due to its simplification. It condenses complex issues and life situations into a single set of principles allowing individuals to more easily perceive and embrace a sense of truth.

Words should be tools to help us think and better understand the world's complexities, not to simplify reality into a set of fixed beliefs about policies or people.

Cult jargon often reinforces the cult identity, as members are trained to internalize the new language and vocabulary. Therefore, with former members of cults, it is crucial to identify the key loaded terms and encourage them to refrain from using them as they can trigger a reversion to their former cult identity.

7. DOCTRINE OVER PERSON

Doctrine over person involves prioritizing the group's beliefs over an individual's personal experience, conscience, and integrity. In an ideologically driven group, opposing worldviews are deemed illegitimate or invalid. The group often defines a common enemy that seeks to disrupt their work, which creates fear and a sense of urgency to accomplish their mission.

The doctrine over person phenomenon occurs when there is a conflict between what one feels oneself experiencing and what the doctrine or dogma says one should experience. If a person's experiences do not align with the doctrine, these experiences are typically ignored or minimized. So, there is a deliberate unhinging of the individual's critical thinking in the cult identity, but critical thinking is still possible when one connects with one's authentic self.

Often, the experience of contradiction can be associated with guilt. One is made to feel that doubts are reflections of the member's immoral nature. Yet doubts can arise, and people may leave the group when conflicts intensify.

8. DISPENSING OF EXISTENCE

Dispensing of existence refers to the belief that only individuals within the group have the right to exist, while ex-members, critics, and dissidents do not. This belief is often symbolic but can lead to dangerous consequences. Those who do not embrace the group's truth are viewed as evil, tainted, and unworthy of existence. In some cults, members who decide to leave are shunned or even killed. Being labeled as someone who does not have the right to exist can cause a person to experience a significant fear of inner extinction or psychological collapse. Conversely, acceptance into the group can bring great satisfaction in feeling part of the elite.

The impulse to draw a sharp line between those who have a right to live and those who do not, which is a totalistic feature, becomes deadly when people are dehumanized and referred to as objects, such as vermin or scum, or defectives. It can justify all types of mistreatment and even lead to death, as it did in the Soviet Union and Nazi Germany.

Cult members are indoctrinated with the belief that if they are expelled from the group or choose to leave, disastrous consequences will befall them. As a result, ex-members are often labeled as "walking dead," spiritually bankrupt, and some cults even consider physical threats, harassment, and murder as acceptable means of dealing with dissenters.

REFLECTIVE EXERCISES

2. Consider Lifton's eight criteria of thought reform and choose one you have personally experienced, either in a mind control group or a "normal" group. Describe your experience. What impact did it have on you at the time?

_____

_____

_____

3. What have you learned from the above experience about the nature of thought reform and the power of group dynamics? Consider how this knowledge can inform your work with clients who have suffered mind control abuse.

4. List some examples of loading the language you have heard used by a political or religious group. What effect do you think this language has?

MARGARET SINGER'S 6 CONDITIONS FOR THOUGHT REFORM

Psychologist Dr. Margaret Singer was another mental health professional tasked to research Chinese Communist brainwashing during the 1950s. She became a leading expert in cult-related legal cases and frequently offered expert witness testimonies.

Singer preferred the term thought reform to mind control or brainwashing. Singer wrote *Cults in Our Midst: The Hidden Menace in Our Everyday Lives*. She presents her model using six conditions to evaluate thought reform or undue influence. These conditions are as follows:

1. Gain control over a person's time, especially their thinking time and physical environment.

Members are often restricted in their access to external information and activities to maintain a singular focus on the group. However, it is worth noting that physical isolation, as was the case with cults in the 1970s to 1990s, is now uncommon. In contemporary times, individuals can be recruited and radicalized online through smartphones, computers, tablets, and television.

2. Create a sense of powerlessness, fear, and dependency while providing models demonstrating the new, ideal behavior.

This tactic involves dismantling a person's sense of self and creating a state of vulnerability and dependency. Cults encourage powerlessness, fear, and dependency while providing examples demonstrating the new, ideal behavior. Behavior control incorporates modeling the "right" behavior for members. Emotional control includes glorifying how "special" and "chosen" the recruit is while manipulating feelings of guilt and leveraging existing fears or installing phobias.

3. Manipulate rewards, punishments, and experiences to suppress the recruit's former social behavior and attitudes, including using altered states of consciousness to manipulate experience.

This tactic involves discouraging or punishing behavior or attitudes inconsistent with the group or individual's ideology. The goal is to inhibit the person's former sense of identity and replace it with a new one aligned with the group or individual's beliefs.

4. Manipulate rewards, punishments, and experiences to elicit behavior and attitudes desired by leadership.

Singer's fourth condition is similar to the third but focuses on behavioral conditioning to strengthen the newly formed cult identity. The cult uses rituals such as group services, studying group ideology, and religious practices like praying, meditating, singing, marching, and bowing, when applicable, to shape the recruit's identity. The aim is to create a sense of obligation to comply with the group's or individual's expectations by programming new behaviors, beliefs, and experiences that reinforce them.

5. Create a tightly controlled system with a closed system of logic, wherein dissenters feel their questioning indicates something inherently wrong with them.

This criterion involves the construction of a belief system that is internally consistent and resistant to external criticism or questioning. The use of circular reasoning, logical fallacies, and other tactics may be employed to persuade the individual that any form of dissent or questioning is a reflection of their moral weakness. For example, although cult ideologies may lack logical coherence, they often have a narrative internally consistent enough for true believers to focus on, disregarding inconsistencies. Totalistic groups may also be described as "self-sealing," employing loaded language to shape thought and prohibiting questioning of the leader, doctrine, or policies.

6. Keep recruits unaware and uninformed that there is an agenda to control or change them. Thought reform is impossible when a person is fully functioning with informed consent.

This tactic involves concealing the true intentions of the group or individual conducting the thought reform and presenting their activities as benign or beneficial. The goal is to prevent the person from realizing they are being manipulated and prevent them from seeking outside help or support. In legal terms, this is a lack of informed consent.

Singer's statement that thought reform is impossible without fully informed consent and total cognitive capacity is powerful. However, it assumes incorrectly that the person is educated about covert hypnotic techniques and other techniques of undue influence.

REFLECTIVE EXERCISES

5. Consider Singer's six conditions for thought reform and choose one you have personally experienced, either in a mind control group or a "normal" group. Describe your experience. What impact did it have on you at the time?

_____

_____

_____

_____

_____

_____

_____

_____

_____

_____

_____

6. What have you learned from the above experience about the nature of thought reform and the power of group dynamics? Consider how this knowledge can inform your work with clients who have suffered mind control abuse.

_____

_____

_____

_____

_____

_____

_____

_____

_____

HASSAN'S BITE MODEL OF MIND CONTROL

The research by Robert Jay Lifton, Margaret Singer, Leon Festinger, and others was pivotal in the development of my BITE Model of Authoritarian Control.

Lifton's eight criteria and Singer's six conditions together offer a valuable framework for understanding critical aspects of the thought reform process. Lifton's perspective is theoretical, borrowing heavily from the identity model of German-American psychologist and psychoanalyst Erik Erikson, and the psychoanalytic tradition derived from Freud. Singer's model offers a more straightforward, more behavioral approach. However, it did not use the dual identity model and missed many important themes and behaviors that have proved helpful for people in cults trying to exit.

The BITE Model identifies and fleshes out specific components that characterize destructive cult policies. For example, the model proposes that behavior, thought, emotion, and information control constitute four overlapping components of mind control. I developed the BITE Model to describe cults' specific methods to recruit and maintain control over people.

Since 1988, tens of thousands of people have reported that The BITE Model has helped them to identify their involvement in a destructive cult, enabling them to exit and reclaim their power. Its value has been demonstrated by individuals involved in various destructive cults and controlling relationships worldwide.

The more criteria present under each component, the more controlling the destructive relationship or group is determined to be.

BEHAVIOR CONTROL

The primary objective of behavior control is to establish reliance on and obedience to the group, its ideology, and its leadership. All significant life choices must be approved or, in some cases, dictated by the group. Failure to obtain permission for important decisions can result in punishment.

Individualism is discouraged, and prioritizing an infallible leader, figurehead, spiritual entity or the group is mandatory. Stringent rules and regulations are imposed and enforced. Thoughts, emotions, and activities (personal or involving others) must be reported to superiors. In unhealthy groups, members' physical reality is regulated - where they live, who they live with, who they associate with, and sometimes who they marry. Typically, members are isolated from anyone perceived to be unsupportive of their involvement with the group.

Cults use various means to enforce conformity, including regulating clothing, hairstyle, living arrangements, diet, and controlling sexuality. Women in some cults, such as the Children of God, are even sent out to work as prostitutes. Members may also be sleep-deprived and financially exploited, often pressured to give up all their wealth and assets and work long hours for the group without pay. Extreme exploitation can be seen in cases of sex trafficking.

Group and self-indoctrination sessions often demand members to dedicate many hours. With the advent of the Internet, cult recruiters now have a 24/7 tool for indoctrination to keep members fully committed. Non-group leisure time, entertainment, or vacation time is limited, and rewards and punishments are doled out for "good" and "bad" behavior. The aim is to discourage individualism and encourage "groupthink." As a result, friends and family members often notice a radical personality shift in the individual.

Corporal punishment, slapping, punching, and hitting with a paddle or belt, is prevalent in some religious groups despite ample research showing that it is never a suitable form of discipline. In the case of sex trafficking, branding and other forms of torture and punishment are also used. Some groups even force members to kill their parents or engage in other extreme acts of violence to ensure their complete obedience. All these tactics aim to create a cult identity that is dependent and obedient.

INFORMATION CONTROL

In ethical groups, newcomers are informed about their beliefs, values, and expectations if they become members. However, unethical groups resort to deceit by lying, concealing crucial information, or altering information to make it seem more acceptable. These tactics undermine the legal right of individuals to have informed consent to make decisions in their best interest.

Cults often work hard to conceal or alter their true history, including the actions of their leaders. Members are frequently unaware of the full extent of wrongdoing in the group's past.

Cults require members to act as spies and report on the thoughts, feelings, and actions of others, including family and friends. Using a buddy system is common, especially when members are out proselytizing, to monitor and control others. Information gathered through formal confessionals or members reporting on each other is used to maintain group control, as seen in Lifton's fourth criterion, The Cult of Confession. False confessions of childhood abuse may be coerced through suggestive counseling or group practices. If a member expresses the desire to leave the group, the leadership may use this information and the threat of disclosure to bring the member back in line.

Mind control groups, particularly political cults, heavily rely on propaganda to influence their members. In the past, propaganda was spread through various mediums such as newsletters, magazines, journals, and audio and video recordings. However, with the advent of the Internet and social media, propaganda is now available 24/7, and meetings are often live-streamed. In addition, prominent groups like Scientology have dedicated publication departments that produce extensive media for its members and the wider public. Usually, the group will quote famous people without their permission and in a way that is out of context to add credibility to their message. Authoritative, trusted figures like doctors, scientists, and other experts are also often asked for comments out of context and then used for propaganda.

Individuals must access information from various reliable sources to think critically and independently. However, cults often condition their members to distrust critics, former members, or media outlets. Some groups go as far as prohibiting their members from reading newspapers, reading books and articles, watching TV, listening to the radio, or accessing science-based information. They also often forbid communication with ex-members of the group.

Furthermore, some controllers keep their followers so occupied that they have no time to investigate or build relationships outside the group. These groups also may control their members' mobile phones by tracking their GPS, sending frequent messages, or calling often. Additionally, some authoritarian groups create multiple "front" groups to obscure their parent organization. Lastly, sleep control and deprivation are often used to keep members exhausted and prevent them from having the time and energy to think or investigate outside the group.

THOUGHT CONTROL

One way of inducing thought reform is using hypnotic and suggestive strategies that create an altered state of consciousness, which can alter a person's thoughts and memories. Unfortunately, these techniques can also create false memories. Other methods of thought control include lengthy, repetitive lectures that require members to memorize and repeat back information, as well as auditory practices such as prayer, chanting, and speaking in tongues. Techniques such as guided meditation and visualization can also implant thoughts and beliefs. These practices discourage critical thinking and make it easier for the group to control its members.

As previously mentioned, the ideology of authoritarian groups tends to be binary, with a clear division between "us" and "them" and a belief in an absolute "truth" that is considered sacred and/or scientific. Members are taught to use "thought-stopping" techniques to prevent impure thoughts and resist feelings that are considered evil. For example, in the Moonies, this was achieved through prayer, chanting, and singing. In other cults, members may speak in tongues or glossolalia, a phenomenon attributed to ancient languages or a divine being speaking through individuals.

Closed groups often develop a language system that outsiders do not share. This includes using "thought-terminating clichés," which reduce complex ideas to simplistic buzzwords known only by other members. While not all groups give members new names, those that do use it as a powerful technique to support changes in the person's identity. Religious cults often tell members to "die to themselves," contributing to the erosion of their authentic selves and forming a new identity that aligns with the cult's image.

Members are discouraged or forbidden from asking critical questions about the leader, doctrine, or organization policies. Rational analysis, critical thinking, and constructive criticism are deemed wrong and can be turned around on a member as a weakness of character or lack of devotion. Other groups and belief systems are portrayed as illegitimate, evil, or invalid.

EMOTION CONTROL

Initially, cult members are often "love-bombed" and flattered, making them feel special and chosen to be part of an elite group. However, this love is conditional on being a good cult member and is quickly withdrawn if a person asks problematic questions or causes trouble. Cults are characterized by extreme emotional highs and lows, with members being showered with love and praise one moment and condemned as sinners the next.

Members are always expected to be grateful and happy, believing they are part of the chosen people who possess the truth and have the key to the world's salvation. Therefore, members often sing songs about the leader, doctrine, or group to maintain positivity or distract themselves from their doubts.

Cult members are taught techniques such as thought-stopping and emotion-stopping to block feelings of homesickness, anger towards leadership, or doubt. Whenever a person experiences negative emotions, they are encouraged to feel guilty and engage in practices to further surrender themselves to the leader or group. Some cults even teach that emotions are evil and must be ignored.

In cults, problems or issues are always blamed on the individual member, while the group and leader are always seen as infallible. Members are sometimes discouraged from experiencing natural emotions, such as sexual attraction or jealousy, and are made to feel guilty and sinful for having them. Likewise, in groups concerned with conventional morality, greed, and envy are labeled as "negative," so members deny and suppress them,

114

often publicly confessing and repenting. This phenomenon can lead to feelings of guilt, unworthiness, and shame, and the group may even try to make members feel guilty for their religion of origin, race, country, or personal history. The cult system creates a constant sense of frustration and dependency, with the group promoting positive self-esteem through membership rather than individual accomplishments.

Emotion control is heavily reliant on guilt and fear tactics in cults. One standard method is phobia indoctrination, which can cause significant harm to an individual's ability to function. Cult leaders either exploit existing phobias or implant them into members' minds, leading them to believe they cannot be happy or fulfilled without the group. Leaving the group is equivalent to non-existence. The phobias can range from spiritual health (such as going to hell or being possessed), physical health (like contracting AIDS or getting killed in an accident), or psychological health (like going insane or being committed to a mental hospital). Fear of the outside world and "enemies" is also common, as well as fear of being shunned or excommunicated by the group, especially for those born and raised in the cult. Members can feel coerced or threatened into staying, even if they no longer believe, out of fear of being labeled "bad" or "sinful" by leadership or losing family and friends. Some members' livelihoods are dependent on remaining in the group. For example members may be employed by the group for many years and rely on other members or leaders for positive employment references.

REFLECTIVE EXERCISES

7. How can mental health professionals use the BITE Model of Authoritarian Control to identify and help individuals affected by undue influence?

_____

_____

_____

_____

_____

8. Reflect on the concept of the authentic self and how it can be suppressed by undue influence. Have you ever felt like you were hiding or suppressing a part of yourself to fit in with a group or organization? Consider how you can connect with your authentic self and be true to yourself, even in challenging situations.

_____

_____

_____

_____

_____

_____

_____

Mind control is a phenomenon that affects individuals around the world. The models discussed in this article have been instrumental in identifying the tactics used by authoritarian groups to gain control over their members. By understanding these models, individuals can recognize the signs of undue influence and protect themselves from falling prey to such tactics. It is important to remember that anyone can be vulnerable to mind control, and it is essential to remain vigilant and informed to prevent such situations. By spreading awareness and knowledge about the techniques used in mind control, we can work towards creating a safer and more informed society.

MODULE 5 RESOURCES

Freedom of Mind Resources

Steven Hassan's BITE Model of Authoritarian Control

Detailed Handout On The Bite Model Of Authoritarian Control

Robert Jay Lifton's Eight Criteria of Thought Reform

Robert Jay Lifton, MD Discusses Trump and His New Book, Losing Reality

Robert Jay Lifton MD: An Interview with a Genius

NXIVM: Robert Jay Lifton's Criteria of Thought Reform as Analyzed by Expert Paul Martin

How Cults Exploit Fervor and Awe to Recruit and Control Members: An Interview With Dr. Yuval Laor

Videos

What is a Cult? Whiteboard Animation Using the BITE Model

Dr. Robert Jay Lifton and Steven Hassan July 13th, 2011

Dr. Robert Jay Lifton and Steven Hassan: August 2012

Steven Hassan interviews Robert Jay Lifton, MD, 9-17-16 (Part 1/3)

Steven Hassan interviews Robert Jay Lifton, MD, 9-17-16 (Part 2/3)

Steven Hassan interviews Robert Jay Lifton, MD, 9-17-16 (Part 3/3)

Books

Thought Reform and the Psychology of Totalism by Robert Jay Lifton

This work delves into the psychological techniques of extreme indoctrination used in various totalitarian regimes, highlighting the profound impact on individual autonomy and belief systems.

Destroying the World to Save It: Aum Shinrikyo, Apocalyptic Violence, and the New Global Terrorism by Robert Jay Lifton

The author examines the motivations and beliefs driving the Aum Shinrikyo cult's deadly actions, shedding light on the intersection of religion, violence, and apocalyptic visions.

Losing Reality: On Cults, Cultism, and the Mindset of Political and Religious Zealotry by Robert Jay Lifton

This analysis explores how cults and extremist groups exploit psychological vulnerabilities to foster unwavering loyalty and zealotry among their followers.

Cults in Our Midst: The Continuing Fight Against Their Hidden Menace by Margaret Singer and Janja Lalich

The book offers a comprehensive look at the recruitment and control tactics employed by cults, providing insights into their pervasive and often hidden influence in society.

Coercive Persuasion: A Socio-psychological Analysis of the "Brainwashing" of American Civilian Prisoners by the Chinese Communists by Edward Schein

     This study investigates the methods of 'brainwashing' employed by Chinese communists on American POWs, offering a critical perspective on the power of coercive persuasion.

When Prophecy Fails: A Social and Psychological Study of a Modern Group that Predicted the Destruction of the World by Leon Festinger, Henry W. Riecken, and Stanley Schachter

     The authors document the aftermath of a failed doomsday prediction, providing a fascinating look into how cognitive dissonance shapes belief revision and group dynamics.

MODULE 6: CULT PSYCHOLOGY

Summary: Explores the psychological dynamics within cults, focusing on manipulation techniques, the effects on members' mental health, and the challenges faced when leaving a cult.

Learning Objectives: To understand the psychological mechanisms used by cults for manipulation; assess the impact of cult involvement on individual mental health; and identify challenges and support strategies for those exiting cults.

Being in a destructive cult that employs mind control techniques and exiting can be an overwhelming and disorienting experience. Individuals in such groups often feel constant mental and emotional turmoil as they struggle to reconcile their thoughts and beliefs with the strict dogma imposed by the organization. The cult's influence permeates every aspect of a member's life, leading them to question their identity and self-worth. The indoctrination process breaks down a person's sense of self, replacing it with a new identity that aligns with the cult's teachings and goals. As a result, members may experience a profound sense of isolation, confusion, and helplessness, feeling trapped in a world where their thoughts and emotions are no longer their own.

Especially when people are born or raised in an authoritarian cult, they are trained to look to the leader and doctrine to tell them what to believe and do. Exiting this highly controlled environment, one often wants to find someone to be that authority. These folks are very susceptible to getting into other authoritarian cults and relationships. Therefore, it is a significant task to help encourage people to think for themselves and make good decisions. This process needs to be developmentally appropriate for the exiting process.

Given the vast array of mind control cults, it is impossible to describe the beliefs and practices of every group. Nevertheless, some aspects of cult involvement tend to be stereotypical. The following are the most frequently encountered themes, and I first described them in *Combating Cult Mind Control*.

Exiting a mind-control cult often leaves individuals disoriented and vulnerable, as their sense of self has been deeply injured. A key part of recovery involves empowering them to reclaim their true identity.

THE DOCTRINE IS REALITY

In an environment dominated by mind control, the group's beliefs are not considered theoretical or open to interpretation. Instead, the doctrine is perceived as the only reality. Moreover, it cannot be verified or evaluated. Some organizations even claim that the entire material world is merely an illusion. Under this view, thoughts, desires, and actions — except those explicitly prescribed by the cult — are designated not to exist.

Doctrine is expected to be accepted rather than comprehended. Therefore, cult members are instructed to adhere to the prescribed principles, often even without a clear understanding. Simultaneously, they are encouraged to put forth more effort and demonstrate greater faith to gain a deeper understanding of the truth. If the doctrine doesn't provide an answer for something directly, then the member must ask a leader or is simply told to try harder to understand.

A group's power stems from its claim of holding the sole and absolute truth. As mind control relies on forging a new identity, the cult's doctrine requires that members distrust their authentic selves. This doctrine becomes the "master program" governing their thoughts, emotions, and actions. Since it is considered the "truth," perfect and infallible, imperfections are attributed to the believer's own shortcomings.

REALITY IS ALL OR NOTHING, US VS. THEM, GOOD VS. EVIL

In mind control organizations, reality is perceived as a pair of binary opposites: all or nothing, us versus them, and good versus evil. There is no space for pluralistic thought or nuance.

The doctrine does not acknowledge the theological validity of any external group, as this would challenge the cult's exclusive hold on the truth. Furthermore, many destructive cults have clearly defined adversaries. These "devils" can differ from one group to another. They may include political or economic institutions (such as communism, socialism, or capitalism), mental health professionals (for example, psychiatrists, psychologists or doctors), or metaphysical entities like Satan, spirits, or aliens. These "devils" are often believed to take on the bodies of parents, friends, ex-members, journalists, and other group critics. The "conspiracies" working against the group prove its immense significance.

REFLECTIVE EXERCISES

1. How do cults use the concept of "devils" or enemies to maintain control over their members and solidify their group identity?

_____

_____

_____

_____

_____

_____

_____

_____

_____

2. How might the perception of reality in binary terms impact a member's relationships with people outside the cult?

_____

_____

_____

_____

_____

_____

_____

_____

_____

_____

3. How might a therapist address and work with a client conditioned to think in binary opposites and us versus them mentalities?

_____

_____

_____

_____

_____

_____

_____

_____

_____

_____

_____

_____

ELITIST MENTALITY

Members are made to feel part of an elite group. This feeling of being "special" and taking on an essential role alongside a dedicated community of believers creates a powerful emotional bond that motivates individuals to continue making sacrifices and working diligently.

Cult members believe they have been selected — by God, destiny, fate, or some other supernatural entity — to guide humanity from darkness into a new era of enlightenment. The closer a member gets to the leader, the more exceptional or chosen they feel. For example, as I advanced in rank and became closer to Moon, I felt increasingly "special" and believed that God was using me at a higher level than others. Cult members often feel they have a mission and hold a unique position in history. Nonetheless, this sense of elitism and destiny comes with a considerable weight of responsibility. Members are informed that failure to execute their duties to the fullest extent equates to failing the entirety of humanity.

The rank-and-file members display humility towards their superiors and prospective recruits but exude arrogance towards outsiders. During recruitment, nearly all members are promised eventual leadership roles. However, progression is contingent upon exceptional performance or political appointment with the cult. Ultimately, the powerful elite remains limited in size. As a result, most members do not ascend to leadership positions, instead continuing as rank-and-file members.

Members of cults perceive themselves as superior, more knowledgeable, and more enlightened than individuals outside their group. Occasionally, they even believe they possess supernatural abilities. For instance, in the higher echelons of Scientology, members see themselves as god-like and think they can manipulate the weather or move objects using their thoughts. They carry themselves with the weight of the world on their shoulders. Simultaneously, they alienate friends and family members, who are made to feel "ignorant" and "inferior" compared to the all-knowing cult member.

Ironically, cult members often express disdain for those involved in other cult groups, sometimes even acknowledging that these individuals are "brainwashed." However, they cannot "step out" of their life situation and objectively look at themselves.

GROUP WILL OVER INDIVIDUAL WILL

Individuals must comply with group policies and the leader's directives in all destructive cults. Cult members often demonstrate a deep commitment to the group's beliefs and values and are willing to make considerable sacrifices to further the group's aims and objectives. As a result, cult members prioritize the group over their own individual needs. In any organization classified as a destructive cult, thinking of oneself or for oneself is considered wrong.

Absolute obedience to superiors is a prevalent theme across cults. Individualism is discouraged, while conformity is encouraged. A cult member's entire sense of reality becomes externally influenced. They learn to dismiss their inner selves and rely on external authority figures for direction and meaning. Cult members tend to seek guidance from others, often struggling with decision-making, likely due to the excessive focus on external authority. In their heightened dependency, they need someone to dictate their thoughts, emotions, and actions.

STRICT OBEDIENCE: MODELING THE LEADER

It is common for cult members to become like clones of their superiors and, ultimately, the cult leader. New members in a cult are often indoctrinated and conditioned to abandon their previous thoughts and behaviors by being paired with a more experienced cult member, who serves as a role model for the newcomer to emulate. In some religious groups, this process is called *shepherding* or *discipling*. The new member is encouraged to become like their mentor. Mid-level leaders are similarly urged to imitate their superiors. The cult leader at the top is, of course, the ultimate model.

Possible reasons a group of cultists might appear peculiar to outsiders are the members' shared odd mannerisms, clothing styles, and speech patterns. The outsider is witnessing the leader's personality reflected in the group. For instance, when I was a member of the

Moonies, I spoke with an accent that was a mix of English, Korean, and Japanese, resulting in awkward English sentences. I essentially became a model of my leader.

HAPPINESS THROUGH GOOD PERFORMANCE

One of the most appealing aspects of cult life is the sense of community it cultivates. Initially, love appears unconditional and boundless, with new members being swept up in a honeymoon phase filled with praise and attention. However, after a few months, as individuals become more entrenched, the flattery and attention are redirected toward newer recruits. Many members still believe their group offers the "highest level" of love on earth. Nevertheless, through their experiences within the group, they learn that love is conditional and dependent on their performance.

Behavioral control is exerted through a system of rewards and punishments. Competitions are employed to motivate and shame members into greater productivity. If the group faces challenges — such as poor recruitment, negative media coverage, or member defections — the blame is placed on individual members, and their share of "happiness" is withheld until the issue is resolved. In some groups, people must confess their sins to be granted "happiness." Ultimately, happiness becomes synonymous with good performance.

Genuine friendships are seen as a liability in cults and are often subtly discouraged by leaders. A cult member's emotional allegiance should be directed towards the leader rather than their peers. A member's friends are usually viewed as a threat to the group, partly because if one member leaves, they might influence others to follow. When someone does leave the group, the "love" that was once directed at them must outwardly transform into anger, hatred, and mockery.

Relationships within cults are typically shallow, as sharing deep personal emotions, particularly negative ones, is strongly discouraged. This superficiality exists even though members may feel closer to their fellow cult members than they have ever felt with anyone else. When cult members experience hardship (e.g., fundraising in extreme weather conditions) or persecution (e.g., facing harassment from outsiders), they often feel an extraordinary sense of camaraderie and shared martyrdom. However, because the only actual loyalty is supposed to be directed towards the leader, a closer examination reveals that these connections exist on a surface level.

REFLECTIVE EXERCISES

4. What are some consequences of a cult member's sense of reality being externally influenced?

_____

_____

_____

_____

_____

_____

_____

_____

_____

_____

_____

5. How does the concept of conditional love contribute to a cult's hold over its members?

_____

_____

_____

_____

_____

_____

_____

_____

_____

_____

MANIPULATION THROUGH FEAR AND GUILT

Cult members often live in a narrow space of fear, guilt, and shame. They constantly believe that any problems they encounter are their own fault, due to personal weaknesses, karma, or doubt. Further, they continuously feel guilty for not meeting the group's standards. As a result, the leader, doctrine, and group are always considered correct, while the members are deemed inherently wrong.

Shame and guilt are employed regularly through various methods, such as praising a particular member for exceptional achievement or identifying issues within the group and attributing them to the members' shortcomings.

In every destructive cult, fear serves as a powerful driving force. Phobias represent the ultimate weapon in the arsenal of mind control. In some cults, members are systematically conditioned to be terrified of leaving the group. Contemporary cults have mastered the art of implanting vivid negative images deep within members' subconscious minds, making them believe that happiness and success are unattainable outside the group. As a result, members are genuinely convinced that leaving the group would result in their destruction, and they believe there is no possibility for personal growth—spiritually, intellectually, or emotionally—outside the group.

When the unconscious is programmed to accept these negative associations, it behaves as if they are true. The unconscious mind of a typical cult member is filled with a vast collection of images depicting the dire consequences that will befall them or others if they betray the group. However, these cult-induced phobias are often so skillfully created and implanted that people may not even be aware of their existence. These phobic thoughts are irrational and frequently nonsensical.

When members become aware of their desire to leave, it's usually just a matter of time before their authentic self develops a stronger voice. Why is this the case? Because mind control groups are continuously altering their doctrines and policies. Members come and go, forcing leaders to lie and change policies to maintain control constantly.

EMOTIONAL HIGHS AND LOWS

Life in a cult can resemble a roller-coaster ride. Members oscillate between the extreme "happiness" of what they experience as the "truth" alongside an exclusive inner circle and the crushing weight of guilt, fear, and shame. These extreme swings contribute to psychological vulnerability and may sometimes lead to misdiagnoses from mental health professionals, such as bipolar disorder. In reality, these fluctuations are manifestations of the mind control state. When members are heightened, they can channel their enthusiasm into remarkable productivity and persuasiveness. However, they may become entirely dysfunctional when they hit a low point. This phenomenon is one reason why mental health professionals should be cautious about hastily medicating or diagnosing someone who has been involved in a mind control cult.

Most cults attempt to block low emotional states to persist in members for extended periods. To this end, some cults require members to undergo reindoctrination programs to rejuvenate their enthusiasm. It is not unusual for an individual to receive formal reindoctrination multiple times each year. Additionally, members are kept occupied and diverted to prevent them from remaining in a low mood for too long. All of these machinations can lead to a suppression of emotional states deemed "bad" or "negative."

When someone leaves a cult, addressing these emotional highs and lows is essential. It's crucial to emphasize that emotions are valuable indicators, and if a client is experiencing shame, they should be encouraged to examine its origins. They should consider whether the feeling resulted from their actions or the environment that induced shame or guilt.

CHANGES IN TIME ORIENTATION

Cults often alter individuals' relationships with their past, present, and future. Members typically view their past through a distorted lens, casting a dark shadow over even the most positive memories. Their perception of the present is also manipulated by the cult, filled with a sense of urgency about the tasks they need to accomplish. For example, many cults teach that the apocalypse is imminent, with some claiming to prevent it while others simply believe they will survive it. When members are consistently occupied with critical projects, their sense of time becomes blurred. For them, the future is when they will receive their reward after the anticipated transformation has occurred.

In most cults, the leader asserts control or claims exclusive knowledge of the future. They craft vivid images of heavenly or hellish futures to steer members in the desired direction. The idea of a perfect and utopian future strongly motivates members to endure discomfort and challenging experiences.

If a cult has an apocalyptic timeline, it is generally set two to five years in the future— distant enough to be imminently discredited but close enough to maintain emotional impact. In many cults, these predictions can sometimes cease to be the focus of attention as the deadline approaches. In other cases, the timetable is believed until the moment it is proven false, after which the leader may issue a new timeline. When this occurs repeatedly, some long-term members may grow cynical. However, new members may be oblivious to the leader's shifting deadlines. Yet in other cases, the belief may deepen. Indeed, people believe *more* if they're asked to hold an extreme belief that, in a lesser form, might be detected as nonsense. Further, the need to believe that a group and its belief systems are working for the greater good can create cognitive dissonance, making it hard to disentangle the incorrect beliefs from the allegedly positive intentions of the group. Finally, the phenomenon of the sunk cost fallacy—in which someone resists acting on good information when they've invested too much in a bad decision—makes it harder to "see the light" and accept it as such, potentially transforming mere believers into fanatics even when their beliefs are more severely challenged.

NO WAY OUT

In the mind of a cult member, there is no valid reason to leave the group. Unlike healthy organizations which acknowledge an individual's inherent right to leave, mind control groups emphasize that leaving is never a legitimate option. Members are taught that the only reasons people leave are weakness, insanity, temptation, brainwashing (by deprogrammers), pride, sin, or any other reasons that implies the member is weak or sinful. Cult members are imbued with the belief that leaving will have terrible consequences for themselves, their families, and/or humanity. This phenomenon helps to explain the age-old question of why people stay. While cult members may claim they would quit if presented with an alternative, they are not granted the time or mental tools necessary to evaluate the evidence objectively. They are trapped in a psychological prison.

This belief—that leaving the cult means forfeiting personal fulfillment and goodness—lies at the core of Lifton's eighth criteria, "Dispensing of Existence," which we covered in the previous module. Dispensing of Existence is the totalistic view that one has the right to exist within the group but loses that right upon leaving. Violent cults may take this approach to an extreme, justifying the killing of former members and reinforcing the idea that people must stay in the group. Members must work, fight, and obey orders, or they will face death—not just symbolically, as in the Moonies—but in reality.

Individuals who leave cults are courageous and can serve a crucial role. They can inspire those still under mind control, particularly when they lead happy, successful lives and openly discuss their cult experiences. These courageous individuals pose a potent threat to cult leaders and mind controllers everywhere by speaking out. Conversely, when former members conceal their cult involvement due to shame, doubt, guilt, fear, or anger, they miss a valuable opportunity to liberate themselves and set an example for others.

In cults, human rights—including the right to question and leave—are not acknowledged. As such, it is necessary for therapists to help clients recognize their human rights and empower them to make life choices for themselves. Members need to understand that there are always valid reasons for leaving a group, such as criminal or immoral actions by the leader or members, finding a healthier organization, or falling in love with a non-member.

I have found that those who were able to leave without intervention were those who had maintained contact with people outside the cult. This communication with outsiders allowed crucial information to penetrate the mental barriers created by the cult, ultimately changing their lives.

REFLECTIVE EXERCISES

6. What are some challenges individuals have leaving a mind control cult?

_____

_____

_____

_____

_____

_____

_____

_____

_____

7. How can former cult members who have successfully left the group serve as a source of inspiration for those still under mind control?

_____

_____

_____

_____

_____

_____

_____

_____

_____

SELECTIVE RECRUITMENT

A common misconception about cult members is that they are weak, unintelligent, uneducated, or mentally ill. In reality, the opposite is often true. Cults typically avoid recruiting those who are seriously ill or with physical or mental challenges, as they don't want members who would be a liability or drain on the group's resources. People with emotional problems may struggle to cope with the group's demanding schedules and intense psychological pressures. Since recruiting and indoctrinating members takes considerable time, energy, and money, cults don't want to waste resources on those who might break down.

Large cult organizations pay attention to cost/benefit ratios like any business. Cults that last more than a decade require competent individuals to manage the practical affairs necessary for long-term objectives. As a result, cults generally target educated, attractive, intelligent, and capable individuals to run their operations, present an excellent public image, and ensure their success.

As discussed in Module 2, anyone, regardless of family background, can be recruited into a cult. The primary factor is not the individual's background but rather a combination of the recruiter's skill and the recruit's current life situation.

ILLUSION OF CHOICE

The illusion of choice occurs when an individual believes they have independently and voluntarily decided to join a group. However, this decision often results from the cult's manipulative recruiting tactics, which frequently are grounded in deception, emotional manipulation, and social pressure.

The potential recruit might think they are making a well-informed and autonomous decision to become a group member, unaware of the underlying motives and the extent of control that will be exercised over them once they join. This false sense of choice strengthens the recruit's commitment to the group, making it more challenging for them to identify and accept that a cult has trapped them. When controlled by a cult, victims may seem content and willing to endure hardships for the benefit or gain of the leader or group.

While they may acknowledge the existence of other cults and brainwashing situations, they remain convinced that their experience is different and that they have not been subjected to the same manipulation.

REFLECTIVE EXERCISES

8. What are some common misconceptions about individuals who join cults, and why are they inaccurate?

_____

_____

_____

_____

_____

_____

_____

_____

_____

_____

_____

_____

The experience of being in a destructive cult that employs mind control techniques can be devastating for individuals. The themes encountered in mind control cults are often universal and include:

- The belief that the doctrine of the group is the only reality;
- Feelings of elitism;
- Group will over individual will;
- An "us versus them" perspective;
- Strict obedience to the leader;
- Manipulation through fear and guilt;
- Happiness through good performance;

- Changes in time orientation;

- Emotional highs and lows, and

- The belief that there is no way out.

While leaving a destructive cult can be difficult, it is possible with the proper support and information.

MODULE 6 RESOURCES

Freedom of Mind Resources

Cult Life: Illusion and Abuse

Stereotypical Profile of Cult Members

Errant Belief #6: "He's Too Intelligent to Join a Cult"

Errant Belief #7: "He Must Be Weak, Stupid, or Looking for Easy Answers or Someone to Tell Him What to Do"

Errant Belief #9: "She'll Walk out on Her Own When She Is Ready"

MODULE 7: IDENTITY CHANGE

Summary: Addresses the process of reconnecting with one's authentic self post-cult involvement, discussing challenges and therapeutic strategies.

Learning Objectives: Guide therapists in supporting clients to rediscover their true selves, facilitating healing from identity fragmentation.

The most significant challenge for individuals who leave destructive authoritarian cults is reconnecting to and growing their authentic identity, while also neutralizing their cult pseudo-identity. Some people have authoritarian (as opposed to authoritative) parents who do not understand how to parent in a developmentally effective way. Healthy identity development aims to help a child grow into an autonomous adult. If parents are members of an authoritarian cult, this creates even more complicated harm. Of course, some people are recruited later in their development. For example, I was nineteen when three attractive women manipulated me into joining the Moon cult. In my case, I had a foundational identity to reorient back to when exiting, but not all exiting members do.

Identity comprises a set of beliefs, behaviors, thought patterns, and emotions that form a distinct sense of self. Under the influence of mind control, a person's core identity is environmentally shaped to conform to and obey authority. Often, children are molded and, in some cases, almost "cloned" by powerful forces. This usually results in a significant identity shift, which substantially disrupts typical identity development. This issue is even more pronounced for children born and raised in a cult, as they are deprived of a psychologically healthy environment to develop, making it more challenging to form a positive sense of self. I believe all humans possess an authentic self that no group can entirely eradicate, leaving hope for genuine healing and the chance to reclaim one's authentic self.

Cults often encourage new recruits to abandon personal relationships, memories, and values, creating a monumental sense of isolation from their previous life.

BORN OR RAISED IN A CULT

While mind control cults can be described in various ways, they are best understood as authoritarian systems that obstruct healthy identity development and functioning.

Children raised in destructive cults do not choose to be a part of these groups; a parent or caretaker makes the decisions for them. However, this choice has a <u>significant impact on their lives</u>. Children affected by high-control groups face many serious issues, including <u>physical, sexual, and psychological harm</u>. There is substantial evidence that corporal punishment is traumatic and causes developmental harm. In addition, destructive cults create an unsafe and abusive environment for children. In addition, other policies and actions might occur, including parental alienation if one parent decides to exit the cult, forced marriage at a young age, lack of proper medical treatment, labor trafficking, sexual predation, and emotional abuse.

The <u>lack of a proper education</u> hinders children's development of critical thinking and reality-testing skills, leaving them vulnerable to mindlessly following whatever leadership tells them to believe and do. When raised in a highly controlled environment, especially from a young age, they struggle to form a healthy sense of self. This is why many adults raised in an authoritarian cult express not knowing who they are or what to believe upon leaving the group. The trauma of being raised in a destructive cult is real and causes long-term harm if not adequately addressed.

CLIENT INTAKE FOR PEOPLE RAISED IN A CULT

Proper initial assessment is crucial for therapists working with clients born or raised in a cult. It is an unfortunate fact that many former or existing cult members can participate in therapy without their therapist ever knowing of their membership. Indeed, understanding a client's specific experience is essential in providing appropriate support and treatment. Each individual's experience within a cult can vary widely, so gathering a comprehensive social history from the client is essential.

I have a <u>form</u> that I ask people to fill out if they can do so, with as much detail as they can. It helps name many of the most common problematic symptoms, as knowing specific areas to address is helpful.

Some key areas to explore during the intake include the client's experience with discipline, corporal punishment, and gender roles. Many religious cults are homophobic, for example. It's also important to ask about the client's education, access to media and technology, and whether they were allowed to have relationships with non-believers. The therapist should also ask about the client's family and childhood experiences, including the age at which their parents joined the cult and whether their parents were also raised within the group.

Additionally, therapists should explore the client's experience with fear-based teachings and end-time prophecies and the group's attitudes towards sexuality, higher education, employment, and marriage.

Here are some questions that would be useful to explore:

- What are the core beliefs and policies of the group?
- Who founded the group, and who leads it now?
- How do they describe their family? Father, Mother? Siblings? Birth order?
- Any major illnesses or deaths?
- Sexual abuse?
- Were they raised in a family or separated and raised communally?
- How was discipline administered?
- Was corporal punishment used (e.g., hand, belt, paddle)?
- Were they forced to watch someone else being corporally punished?
- Did punishment vary depending on the status or whim of leadership?
- Were there strict gender roles and strict parent/child roles?
- Were they raised communally or in a nuclear family?
- Do they have contact with extended family members?
- How old were their parents when they joined? What was their childhood like?
- How were sex and sexuality talked about, if at all? What were sexuality practices in the cult?
- Were they home-schooled, or exposed to public education? Were science, math, and liberal arts included in the curriculum? What was emphasized and omitted?
- Were play, imagination, and fantasy encouraged?
- Were clients allowed to connect with others outside of your group?
- Did the group teach fear about the End Times, Last Days, or Armageddon?
- Was there discouragement from higher education?
- Were women treated as second-class? What were the beliefs around pregnancy and birth?
- Was there a special dispensation if someone was wealthy or famous?
- Was there a strict hierarchy within the group?
- Was there access to media, the internet, books, and libraries?

By gathering this information during intake, therapists can better understand clients' experiences and provide more effective support and treatment.

RECLAIMING THE AUTHENTIC SELF

Over the decades, many people born into prominent cults—the Moonies, Scientology, Hare Krishna, Children of God, Transcendental Meditation (TM)—began coming of age and questioning the programming they received from their groups. This questioning and breaking free from the group's influence is often challenging and painful, but it can lead to a renewed sense of identity and purpose.

When a client expresses uncertainty about their identity, therapists can ask questions such as, "When do you feel the most you?" and "Who would you like to be in the future?" to encourage them to have some reference points.

If they are unsure how to answer, therapists can further explore their interests, hobbies, and values to help them discover their true passions and desires. For instance, therapists can ask clients about favorite activities such as dancing, singing, art, sports, or spending time in nature. They can also ask them to identify individuals they admire who are not affiliated with the cult and explore their inspiring qualities. Additionally, therapists can inquire about any characters in books or movies that clients respect and ask what they appreciate about those characters. By encouraging clients to explore their interests and values, therapists can help them develop a new identity based on authenticity and honesty with themselves.

Therapists can encourage clients to view life as a journey of self-discovery rather than a destination. Uncovering one's authentic self is ongoing, and no single "correct" version of oneself exists. Through this process of self-exploration, clients can learn to identify their core values and beliefs and develop a stronger sense of self-worth and identity.

Therapists need to emphasize the client's agency in this process, as they are the ones who ultimately determine who they want to be. Therapists can provide guidance and support, but it is up to the client to make the choices that align with their authentic self.

While there is no scientific way to prove it, I believe humans are born with an authentic self and a natural desire for love, fairness, truth, and meaning. While this authentic self may not have been fully nurtured and developed, it is a deep-seated aspect of a person's genetic makeup that no one can erase. As a result, there is always hope for healing and even creating one's identity.

CASE STUDY — FRANCES PETERS: BORN AND RAISED IN THE WATCHTOWER SOCIETY, OTHERWISE KNOWN AS THE JEHOVAH'S WITNESSES

Frances Peters' story is one of courage, resilience, and perseverance. Raised from infancy in the Jehovah's Witnesses, she was surrounded by an environment where strict adherence to doctrine was the norm.

Frances' mother became a Jehovah's Witness when Frances was a baby, but her father never converted, causing a divide within the family. Nevertheless, Frances attended meetings with her mother from a young age and, at 15, was baptized into the group. Her sisters were also members, providing a built-in support system for staying within the group's boundaries.

As Frances grew older, she and her family became more devoted, focusing on preaching as much as possible to avoid having "blood on their hands." The Jehovah's Witnesses believe that preaching is necessary to save as many souls as possible before the end of the world, which they are taught to believe is imminent.

When Frances was 13, her parents separated. Frances' mother became even more devoted to the group after the separation as the elders stepped in under the guise of support. Despite her brothers and father not becoming Jehovah's Witnesses, Frances and her sisters remained devoted.

The harsh doctrines of the Jehovah's Witnesses include beliefs that every other church is evil. No birthdays or holidays are celebrated. Blood transfusions are prohibited. The group is homophobic. It also has had a policy for decades which has worked to protect pedophiles rather than reporting them to the police, prosecuting them, or exiling them to protect children. To cement its grip on the member, the group installs phobias of Armageddon, a moment they teach can occur at any second. This carefully designed belief discourages activities such as having children, attending college or higher education, or focusing on a career.

At age 20, Frances married her childhood friend and fellow Jehovah's Witness. After 11 years of marriage, they had their first child, which caused Frances to reevaluate her beliefs. Previously, she and her husband had focused solely on preaching, working just enough to get by—enough for food and basics. However, as she began to explain the concepts of the cult to her children, Frances realized how irrational they sounded.

Her husband also began to doubt, especially when they considered what they would do if one of their children needed a blood transfusion. Frances recalls the first time her husband raised doubts about the Jehovah's Witnesses, discussing his findings with her about the organization having NGO (Non-governmental organization) status. Frances remembers feeling as though it couldn't be true, but her husband was able to prove it, and that began the journey to freedom for their family.

While Jehovah's Witnesses preach an anti-government stance, they maintain NGO (non-governmental organization) status to gain financial and institutional benefits.

As soon as Frances realized how controlling and harmful the group was, she decided to leave. However, speaking up about her concerns led to her being <u>disfellowshipped</u>, a common practice among many extreme cults. Disfellowship meant that she and her husband were banished. Any of their friends and family still within the Jehovah's Witnesses were forbidden from interacting with them.

Shunning is indeed a very powerful form of social control. Losing one's entire network at a single moment can be highly traumatizing. For Frances, losing her family members caused a significant identity crisis, as she had been born into the group and did not have an identity or value system to return to. Despite this, Frances found the courage to leave the group, though the process was complicated. It was a significant benefit that she and her husband left together with their children. Often, one parent leaves, the remaining parent keeps the children in the cult, and the cult works to create a dynamic of parental alienation.

After leaving the Jehovah's Witnesses, Frances found that she was emotionally immature, had difficulty making decisions, and lacked a sense of self. However, spending time with people outside the cult helped her grow and develop a new identity. She also recognized a gap in the knowledge base of professionals around growing up in cults and the harm this can cause to identity development. As a result, Frances was motivated to help others struggling with the same issues, and she went on to gain counseling qualifications. Today, she runs her own self-employed coaching and counseling practice called Free Choice Recovery and Stronger After.

Listen to Frances Peters describing her experience growing up in the Jehovah's Witnesses here.

REFLECTIVE EXERCISES

1. How did being raised in a cult affect Frances' identity development?

_____

_____

_____

_____

_____

_____

_____

_____

2. How did being disfellowshipped affect Frances' sense of self?

_____

_____

_____

_____

_____

_____

_____

_____

_____

_____

_____

_____

3. Consider the impact of being born or raised in a cult on a person's identity. How might this differ from the experience of someone recruited into a cult?

_____

_____

_____

_____

_____

_____

_____

_____

_____

_____

_____

CLIENT INTAKE FOR PEOPLE RECRUITED INTO A CULT

When conducting an intake with clients recruited into a cult, the process will differ from that used for individuals born or raised in a cult. The intake form is the same one for those born into a cult. It helps name many of the most common symptoms, so knowing specific areas to address is helpful. It is also essential to understand the client's concept of recruitment, as some individuals may not recognize that they were deceptively recruited. They might mistakenly believe that they freely chose to join the group.

Recruiters also use a common toxic belief to make people believe there is no such thing as victims or coincidence. Followers are programmed to believe that they created their "reality." This can mean that if they were raped or mugged, they are told that their "soul" created this experience for themselves so they could learn from it. Of course, this belief is nonsense, as it justifies any act and morality ceases to exist.

The therapist should also ask about the recruitment process, including how the client was initially approached (e.g., via an online platform, video, in-person, through a friend or family member); their commitments to the group; and any pressure they experienced to recruit others. When a member recruits someone to enter the cult, it solidifies their commitment to the group.

It is also important to unpack the client's experience within the cult, including the level of isolation they experienced, the time commitment required by the group, and whether someone with power or influence recruited them. Therapists should ask whether these individuals are still in the client's life and whether any family members in the cult have left or are still active members. Understanding the client's interactions with former cult members is crucial. Some individuals may experience pressure and guilt when interacting with these individuals, potentially hindering their ability to move forward in their healing process.

As discussed, my BITE Model of Authoritarian Control helps to identify and flesh out specific components that characterize destructive cult experiences. I recommend directing clients to the Influence Continuum and BITE Model, asking them to fill out their experience. The therapist can also provide examples whenever possible.

Conducting an intake with clients recruited into a cult requires a sensitive and nuanced approach. By understanding the client's recruitment process and experience within the group, therapists can provide tailored support and guidance designed to meet the client's unique needs and circumstances.

THREE STAGES OF GAINING CONTROL OF THE MIND

A three-stage model describing the process of gaining control of someone else's mind was derived in the late 1940s from the work of Kurt Lewin and was described in Edgar

Schein's 1961 book *Coercive Persuasion*. Schein, like Lifton, studied the brainwashing programs in Mao Tse Tung's China in the late 1950s. Based on an interview with former American prisoners, his book is a valuable study of the process. Schein's three stages — unfreezing, changing, and refreezing — apply just as well to other forms of mind control as they do in brainwashing. As he described, unfreezing consists of breaking a person down; changing constitutes the indoctrination process; and refreezing builds up and reinforces the new identity.

These three steps are crucial to understanding how authoritarian cults operate and create a new identity (the "cult self") in their members. Although the "real self" is never destroyed, it is suppressed by the cult self, resulting in a radical personality change that is noticeable to the family and friends of the individual.

As outlined in Module 1 and Module 4, maintaining a dual identity creates a dissociative disorder, as described in the DSM-V-TR, (F44.89):

> *Identity disturbance due to prolonged and intense coercive persuasion: Individuals who have been subjected to extreme coercive persuasion (e.g., brainwashing, thought reform, indoctrination while captive, torture, long-term political imprisonment, recruitment by sects/cults or by terror organizations) may present with prolonged changes in, or conscious questioning of, their identity.*

The three stages of gaining control of the mind are described below.

1. UNFREEZING

In the first stage, a recruit's psychological stability is disrupted to confuse and disorient them, preparing them for radicalization. This technique is done through various techniques that systematically create confusion and self-doubt, disorienting and assaulting the individual's beliefs and ways of making sense of the world.

Unfreezing is most effectively accomplished in a totally controlled environment, like an isolated country estate. Still, it can also be achieved in more familiar and easily accessible places, such as a coffee shop.

DISORIENTATION AND CONFUSION

Humans unconsciously learn and adapt to their environment. In fact, most information influences people without conscious analysis. Therefore, indoctrinators must shake up a person's view of reality to disarm their natural defenses against new concepts that challenge this reality. One way to accomplish this in someone else is to disorient and confuse them. This process challenges their frames of reference, which would otherwise help them to understand themselves and their surroundings.

SENSORY DEPRIVATION AND OVERLOAD

Sensory deprivation or overload can disrupt a person's balance and increase their susceptibility to suggestion. Sleep deprivation is one of the most common and powerful techniques for breaking a person down. Conversely, overloading a person with emotionally laden material at a rate that exceeds their ability to process creates a sense of being overwhelmed. As a result, their mind will stop evaluating the information being presented. The newcomer may think this is happening spontaneously within themselves, but the cult has intentionally structured it that way.

PSYCHOLOGICAL MANIPULATION

Controlling a person's sleep, diet, use of drugs, and level of privacy, as well as minimizing time and resources that encourage reality testing can be very disorienting. This process is relatively fast and easy because humans are more vulnerable when tired, isolated, and deprived of basic needs.

HYPNOSIS

Hypnosis is a powerful technique that can be used to sidestep an individual's defense mechanisms and facilitate the process of unfreezing. One such technique is the deliberate use of confusion to induce a trance state, which involves communicating contradictory information in a congruent manner. This technique can result in a state of temporary confusion. Over time, individuals may suspend their critical judgment and adapt to what others are doing, thereby increasing their susceptibility to suggestions.

Double binds are another hypnotic technique that can help unfreeze a person's sense of reality. This technique involves forcing a person to do what the controller wants while giving an illusion of choice. For example, a cult leader may say, "For those having doubts about what I am telling you, you should know that I am the one putting those doubts inside your mind so that you will see the truth that I am the true teacher." This creates a situation in which the individual is only left with two choices which ultimately lead to the same conclusion.

Guided meditations, personal confessions, prayer sessions, vigorous calisthenics, and group singing are all exercises that can aid unfreezing. Initially innocuous, these activities gradually become more intense and directed over time. They are often conducted in groups, which enforces privacy deprivation and thwarts the person's need to be alone and reflect. In addition, cults may use this opportunity to bombard individuals with the idea that they are seriously flawed, mentally ill, or spiritually fallen, further undermining their sense of self-identity.

Age regression is another powerful mind-altering technique that can disorient individuals and make them more compliant. It involves leading the person to believe they have returned to childhood, effectively putting them in a childlike mindset. When a person is in a hypnotic trance, the mind can be hijacked with false beliefs implanted into their unconscious. For example, cults may program individuals to believe that the cult leaders are their parents, which creates a sense of dependence and increases the individual's susceptibility to suggestion.

Storytelling is another powerful tool for indoctrination that often takes place over several hours or days, forcing the recruit to conform and comply with group authority. Questioning the individual's self-identity and beliefs makes them more malleable and easier to change. In addition, cult leaders may embed messages or metaphors within their stories to disorient the listener and reinforce the cult ideology.

GETTING THE PERSON TO QUESTION SELF-IDENTITY

Once the individual's sense of reality is disturbed, they begin to question their sense of self-identity. This process is essential because people must be willing to redefine themselves, making their beliefs and behaviors easier to change.

REDEFINING THE INDIVIDUAL'S PAST

Indoctrinators can manipulate and redefine an individual's past, including implanting false memories and intentionally causing the individual to forget positive ones. This often involves gaslighting, a technique that deliberately disrupts a person's memory and can lead to the individual questioning their sanity.

USE OF DRUGS AND ALCOHOL

Some cults use drugs or alcohol to facilitate the unfreezing process. Substances are used to lower inhibitions, impair judgment, and create confusion or euphoria, making the individual less likely to resist the group's indoctrination and more susceptible to suggestion and questioning their identity.

2. CHANGING

The second stage is indoctrination. Changing consists of instilling a new personal identity— a new set of behaviors, thoughts, and emotions— to fill the void left by the breakdown of the old identity. Behaviors are shaped subtly at first, then more forcefully as the individual becomes more accepting of the new identity. Finally, the group gives the individual the material they are deemed ready to assimilate. This gradual and controlled approach helps to ensure that the individual becomes fully immersed in the cult's ideology and beliefs.

FORMAL AND INFORMAL INDOCTRINATION SESSIONS

Indoctrination in this new identity occurs formally (for instance, through seminars and rituals) and informally (by spending time with members, reading, and listening to recordings and videos). The new belief system and code of conduct are taught during these sessions, with the person often paired up with an older group member to learn and model proper cult behavior. Many of the same techniques used in the unfreezing phase are also carried into this phase.

REWARD AND PUNISHMENT

Common strategies to change identity include behavior modification techniques to shape and reinforce specific behaviors while punishing others. This process is achieved through a system of rewards, such as praise, promotion, or compensation for compliance while punishing those who disregard them. The cult always seeks to control the member's environment as much as possible.

MYSTICAL MANIPULATION

Mystical manipulation, one of Robert Jay Lifton's eight criteria (see Module 5), is a hallmark of thought reform environments. Destructive cults, especially those with religious leanings, often use this tactic to convince their followers that the leader possesses supernatural abilities such as mind-reading or prophecy. However, these abilities are typically an illusion, achieved by gathering information from other sources—a process unbeknownst to the member. As a result, when predictions come true, individuals mistakenly believe they follow a divine entity. One example of this technique in action is Sai Baba, an Indian guru who had millions of followers convinced that he could manifest objects like a Rolex watch out of thin air. In reality, he used sleight of hand to create the illusion.

HYPNOSIS AND MIND-ALTERING TECHNIQUES

During the changing phase, hypnotic and mind-altering techniques are often employed to mold the new cult identity. Repetition, monotony, and rhythm are used to reinforce the new beliefs and behaviors. Chanting, praying, and decreeing are also used to create a hypnotic state in which the new ideas are easily absorbed. In some groups, members are collectively instructed to verbally affirm rules and beliefs aloud on a consistent basis. Visualizations, affirmations, cult songs, and recitations can effectively program new beliefs. New postures and physical behaviors reinforce the new identity. These techniques are often used with behavior modification techniques, such as rewards and punishments, to ensure compliance with the new belief system. The goal is to create a new identity consistent with the cult's ideology.

CONFESSION AND TESTIMONIALS

Confession and testimonials are a powerful way to manipulate individuals into conforming to the cult's ideals and norms. Group sharing sessions are utilized, where members confess their past evils, share present success stories, and foster a sense of community. These sessions effectively teach conformity, as the group reinforces certain behaviors with effusive praise and acknowledgment while punishing non-group ideas and behaviors with icy silence. In addition, members may share their stories of transformation, detailing how their life was miserable before joining the group and how much happier they are now that they have abandoned their old ways. These personal stories are a powerful tool to influence others and encourage them to conform to the group's beliefs and behaviors.

Human beings have an incredible capacity to adapt to new environments. Charismatic cult leaders know how to exploit this strength. By controlling a person's environment, using behavior modification to reward some behaviors and suppress others, and inducing hypnotic states, they may reprogram a person's identity. Once a person has been thoroughly broken down through the changing process, they are ready for the next step.

3. REFREEZING

The recruit must now be built up again as a new person. They are given a new purpose in life and activities that will solidify their new identity. Cult leaders must be reasonably sure the new cult identity will remain intact even after the recruit leaves the immediate cult environment. This requires the recruit to fully internalize the new values and beliefs to strengthen their newfound identity.

Many techniques from the first two stages are carried over into the refreezing phase. The recruit's first and most important task is to disavow their previous "sinful" self and adopt the new cult identity. Acting like the old self is discouraged, while imitating the new cult self is praised. The new identity is often fully developed in a short time, sometimes within a matter of days or months.

The process of refreezing involves the suppression of their old identity while the new identity is established. This new cult identity often includes a new name, clothes, tattoos, or even a new language or family. The recruit is paired with an older member who serves as a model of behavior for the new member to follow. This helps keep the more senior members on their best behavior and gratify their egos while motivating the new members to strive to become respected models themselves. As the new identity is established, the person feels reborn and begins to imitate the behavior of their spiritual model in all ways.

In refreezing, the separation from the past may entail the destruction of old photographs, videos, or any memorabilia associated with the former identity. The indoctrination process continues, with mandatory group functions scheduled to occupy many hours a week, including workshops and studying group beliefs, values, and activities. Money and possessions are often donated to the cult. The group functions not only as a means of occupying the member's time but also as a tool for further indoctrination and recruitment of new members. Some groups send members out to fundraise as well as recruit. The goal is to maintain members' commitment to the group and prevent backsliding into the old identity.

During this final phase, the person's memory undergoes distortion, with positive memories from the past being minimized and their sins, failings, hurt, and guilt amplified. The cult requires individuals to abandon their special talents, interests, hobbies, friends, and family. Confession is another tool used to cleanse the individual's past and cement their commitment to the group.

REFLECTIVE EXERCISES

4. Consider the three stages of gaining control of the mind. Have you ever experienced these techniques being used on you, whether in a cult or other situation? How did it affect you?

_____

_____

_____

_____

_____

_____

_____

_____

_____

_____

5. Reflect on your own experiences with group dynamics. Have you ever felt pressure to conform to the beliefs or behaviors of a group? How did you handle that pressure, and what did you learn from the experience?

_____

_____

_____

_____

_____

_____

_____

_____

_____

_____

_____

6. Think about the importance of building a sense of community and belonging in our lives. How do we balance the need for community with individuality and self-expression?

_____

_____

_____

_____

_____

_____

_____

_____

_____

_____

_____

THE DUAL IDENTITY MODEL

In a mind-controlled environment, the old identity is not erased but instead suppressed by the new cult identity. Robert Jay Lifton referred to this process as "doubling" in his 1986 book *The Nazi Doctors*.

Although people generally choose what they believe is best for them when given the freedom of choice, the ethical criteria for determining what is best should come from one's values and beliefs rather than from external sources. In a mind-controlled environment, freedom to choose is often lost, and the individual operates within the artificial cult identity structure that replaces their original beliefs. In such an environment, the cult leader's doctrine becomes the absolute truth, creating a new reality for the members.

CONFLICT BETWEEN THE AUTHENTIC SELF AND THE CULT SELF

Members of a mind control cult often feel intense inner conflict, torn between their authentic self and their cult self. This dual identity model is important to remember when interacting with a cult member, as their actions and beliefs may be heavily influenced by their cult identity rather than their true self. Furthermore, this duality extends to those born into destructive cults, as they are raised from a young age with the beliefs and practices of the group but may struggle to reconcile their thoughts and feelings with those of the cult.

Relatives and friends of cult members can find it challenging to identify and deal with these dual identities. This confusion is particularly common during the initial weeks or months of the person's involvement in the cult, as their new identity is more pronounced during this period. Sometimes, the person will speak using cultic jargon and exhibit a hostile or elitist know-it-all attitude, only to abruptly switch back to their old self with their previous attitudes and mannerisms. However, this shift is temporary, as they quickly revert to their cult identity. The cult identity typically dominates the individual's personality, with their old self appearing only sporadically.

THE AUTHENTIC SELF SURVIVES

Even though cult indoctrination attempts to eliminate the old identity and establish a new one, it rarely succeeds one hundred percent. Positive experiences and memories do not disappear entirely. The cult identity may try to suppress the person's past and bury their former life, but eventually, the old self will emerge and strive to regain freedom. This process is accelerated by positive interactions with non-members and the accumulation of negative experiences within the group. The true identity — the core self beneath the mind control virus — sees and records contradictions and disillusioning experiences and brings out questioning or reality-testing of the experience.

An essential part of counseling a client who is still trapped in a cult is to help them access their real self and then integrate the parts of the authentic identity co-opted by the cult identity. The goal is to restore the creative, interdependent, authentic self and enable the individual to digest and integrate their experience and become stronger.

REFLECTIVE EXERCISES

7. Reflect on the importance of helping clients access their authentic selves. How can you support them in this process?

_____

_____

_____

_____

_____

_____

_____

_____

_____

_____

_____

_____

The disruption of authentic identity is a significant challenge faced by individuals who leave destructive cults. This issue is particularly pronounced for those born and raised in cults who were deprived of a psychologically healthy environment for development. However, all human beings possess an authentic self that cannot be entirely eradicated by any group, offering hope for healing and the chance to reclaim one's true identity.

MODULE 7 RESOURCES

Freedom of Mind Resources

Growing up in a Sex Cult with Former Army Captain Daniella Mestyanek Young

Born Into And Married In The Moon Cult With Elgen Strait

Children are Harmed by Destructive Cults — Part One

Children are Harmed by Destructive Cults: Part Two

From Growing Up in the Jehovah's Witnesses to Counseling People Who Wish to Exit it with Frances Peters

The BITE Model and Jehovah's Witnesses

How Jehovah's Witness Teachings Can Damage Brain Development in Children

Shunning and the BITE Model of Mind Control in the Jehovah's Witnesses

Videos

The Freedom of Mind Approach to Helping Individuals Born in High-Demand Groups and Cults

From Growing Up in the Jehovah's Witnesses to Counseling People Who Wish to Exit It with Frances Peters

Websites

Advocates for Awareness of Watchtower Abuses

Ex-Scientology Kids

Books

Beyond Belief: My Secret Life Inside Scientology and My Harrowing Escape by Jenna Miscavige

The authors document the aftermath of a failed doomsday prediction, providing a fascinating look into how cognitive dissonance shapes belief revision and group dynamics.

<u>Coercive Persuasion by Edgar Schein</u>

This book delves into the study of mind control and reeducation techniques, particularly those used during the Korean War, to understand the mechanisms of thought reform.

<u>Educated: A Memoir by Tara Westover</u>

This memoir narrates the author's transformative journey from growing up in a strict, survivalist family to pursuing an education that opened new worlds and ways of thinking.

MODULE 8: HOW TO HELP: PSYCHOEDUCATION EMPOWERING PEOPLE TO BECOME THEIR AUTHENTIC SELF

Summary: Emphasizes psychoeducation in aiding individuals affected by cults, focusing on educating clients about the nature of cult influence.

Learning Objectives: Empower clients through enhanced understanding of their experiences, enabling them to regain control and make informed decisions about their well-being.

In Module 8 of this course, the focus shifts towards therapeutic strategies and considerations for helping individuals impacted by cult experiences.

The lack of training for therapists in identifying and addressing the specific after-effects of cult experiences is a common issue. Many individuals have reported feeling frustrated with needing to educate their therapists about cults and working with cult victims. The responsibility falls on therapists to obtain the necessary training and supervision to assist those impacted by cult experiences. While learning from each client is a natural part of the work, therapists must prioritize understanding the centrality of this issue and take the necessary steps to become more knowledgeable and skilled.

My approach to cult recovery is based on my personal journey and my first-hand experience with being recruited into a cult, becoming a leader, nearly dying, and ultimately being deprogrammed. In this module, I share with therapists what I have learned through this process and from over 45 years of experience empowering individuals to become their authentic selves through the therapeutic process.

CLIENT-CENTERED PSYCHOTHERAPY

Client-centered psychotherapy is an approach that prioritizes the client's perspective and model of the world rather than imposing the therapist's viewpoint. Everyone is unique and has a particular way of understanding and interacting with reality. Therefore, I constantly adjust myself to fit each specific client's needs.

In my approach to client-centered psychotherapy, I draw inspiration from pioneers such as psychiatrist Milton Erickson, who specialized in therapeutic hypnosis and family therapy, and Carl Rogers, who prioritized unconditional positive regard and understanding the client's unique experiences. Additionally, I incorporate Murray Bowen's family systems therapy and David Burns' approach, which encourages clients to gain insight into their thoughts, feelings, and behaviors.

To effectively practice this approach, a counselor must thoroughly understand the client—their values, needs, wants, and thought processes. Then, by temporarily stepping into the client's perspective, a therapist can help their client better understand what *they* want to do. This approach is based on the premise that, deep down, even the most dedicated cult members desire to leave.

My approach to therapy has also been influenced by my extensive training in dissociative disorders by a number of top experts. The Structured Clinical Interview for DSM-IV Dissociative Disorders (SCID-D), created by psychiatrist Marlene Steinberg is considered the gold standard for clinical evaluation of dissociative disorders. The SCID-D is a diagnostic tool used to assess and categorize the presence and severity of dissociative disorders. These disorders often involve a fragmentation of identity, memory, or consciousness, which parts therapy aims to address by fostering a more cohesive sense of self.

I first learned how to utilize "parts" therapy—taught by Virginia Satir—in the early 1980s when I was first learning NLP. Parts therapy is a therapeutic approach that identifies and addresses various facets or "parts" of a person's psyche. It operates on the premise that our personality is composed of numerous parts, each with its own perspective, feelings, and memories. By communicating with these parts, therapists aim to resolve internal conflicts and promote psychological harmony.

Richard Schwartz wrote a book on Internal Family Systems (IFS) which has become almost cult-like in its method of multi-level marketing of therapists to attain certification. In recent years, I have heard disconcerting things about the overreliance of this approach that has caused harm to clients.

In my work with families wishing to be coached in how to help their loved ones who are involved in authoritarian groups or relationships, I highly recommend getting trained in family systems approaches. I recommend structural as well as strategic family therapy approaches. I have primarily utilized strategic theory and methodology to help families extricate individuals from cults.

When an individual is involved in a destructive cult, it is not just the individual who is affected but also their family and friends. In my approach, involving the family and friends of the individual is crucial in the recovery process. You can train the family to communicate more effectively with the cult member. Often, they first need to do "damage control" and repair hurt feelings to develop rapport and trust. Teaching active listening skills is vital. When the affected person feels genuinely "heard," that sets the foundation for being able to ask respectful questions to promote reality testing. However, this approach demands a lot from the family, including a willingness to learn new ways of communicating and resolving existing issues.

When the focus is on the family, positive changes can occur. The cult member becomes aware of positive things happening outside the cult, while family members learn how to build rapport and trust and plant questions in the cult member's mind. A healthy family's love supports an individual's right to grow into an autonomous adult and make their own life decisions. In contrast, a cult's love seeks to keep individuals dependent and may be withdrawn if they fail to follow the leader's orders. A family's unconditional love is a much stronger force than the conditional love given by cult leaders.

As a therapist, I provide a supportive and non-judgmental environment where clients can explore their issues and work toward personal growth and development. By prioritizing the client's unique perspective and experiences, I seek to actively empower individuals to participate in their therapy and achieve positive outcomes.

A SPECIALIZED APPROACH: ASSESSMENT AND TREATMENT STEPS

Recovering from the effects of undue influence requires a specialized approach to assessment and treatment. To ensure the safety and well-being of the client, the therapist must first conduct a thorough history so an accurate evaluation of the client's experiences and the impact on their psychological state can be accomplished.

These are the steps I recommend:

1.　*Intake Form* - When I am contacted by an individual seeking recovery services, I ask them to fill out a <u>Case Evaluation Form</u>. The form includes fields for personal information, details about the controlling group or individual, and additional information about the client's history, health, and current situation. The form also asks about the client's current challenges, family and social network, and actions they have already taken to obtain help. The purpose of the form is to provide a structured and organized way for clients to communicate their experiences and needs to the therapist. The information guides the initial consultation with the client. Then, I provide recommendations for the next steps, including strategies, intervention services, post-intervention recovery resources, and other resource and referral options.

2.　*Safety Assessment* — Assess whether the client is in danger and has their basic needs met.

3.   *Build Trust* — Establish clear agreements for working together. Explain that they are free to share their feelings, disagree with the therapist, give feedback, and ask questions.

4.   *Explore* — Explore the client's current situation, such as whether they maintain involvement with the controlling group or individual or if they need to make an exit plan.

5.   *Psychoeducation* — Provide education about mind control at the beginning and continue incorporating it throughout the therapeutic process.

6.   *Assess for trauma* — Learn more about the client's experiences in the cult and childhood and establish whether there are specific instances of trauma.

7.   *Healing and recovery* — Help the client to develop skills that facilitate recovery.

THERAPEUTIC CONSIDERATIONS

Working with former cult members requires specific therapeutic considerations to address their unique challenges and experiences. These considerations must prioritize the client's safety and capacity to meet their basic needs. When the client's current situation is stable, therapy can move towards exploring their experiences in greater depth and then helping them develop skills that facilitate their healing and recovery. The following points should be considered when working with former cult members:

IS THE CLIENT SAFE?

Prioritizing the safety of clients is of utmost importance. One crucial aspect of ensuring safety is determining whether someone in their life is actively harming them. If such a situation is found, it is essential to assist clients in developing an exit strategy and identifying resources to ensure their safety. This may include finding a safe place to stay and financial support to sustain them during this period. Once the client is out of danger, they can begin therapy to help them cope with the aftermath of the experience. Safety and security should always come first, and therapists must be vigilant in assessing potential risks to their clients.

ARE THEY STILL IN CONTACT WITH THE CULT IN ANY WAY?

Therapists must know whether a client is still actively involved in a cult. They may either be considering leaving or still fully immersed in their "cult identity," making it difficult to acknowledge any negative aspects of the group. Thus, assessing the client's current situation is essential to determine their level of involvement in the cult and provide appropriate support and guidance.

There may be cases in which a client has been cut off from their support network of family and friends who remain within the cult, leaving them without any resources or support network. As a result, they may be too afraid to contact a family member for help. In such situations, the therapist can act as an intermediary with the client's written permission. The therapist can identify a family member who is most likely to be responsive to an appeal for help and offer to call to help the client access necessary resources and support. This can be a vital step towards helping clients find a safe place and get the help they need.

DO THEY HAVE THEIR BASIC NEEDS MET?

It is essential to determine whether the client has access to food, shelter, and income to meet their basic needs, as this can significantly impact their mental health and overall well-being. If the client's basic needs are met, it will be easier for them to focus on the therapeutic process and make progress toward their goals. Therapists must work with clients to identify barriers preventing them from meeting their basic needs and help them access necessary resources to ensure their safety and stability.

ARE THEY STILL DOING CULT PRACTICES?

Some people continue to perform cult practices and rituals. Others might visit the cult website, messaging platform, or social media sites. Some people exit a controlling, abusive relationship but continue going to the person's social media.

Therapists must establish if clients are still engaged in cult practices after leaving. Such practices may include behaviors such as bowing to an altar with the cult leader's picture on it or practicing the same hypnotic meditation techniques they were taught in the cult. Identifying these practices can help the therapist understand the extent of the former member's attachment to the cult and the ongoing influence of its teachings. Through therapy, clients can identify these behaviors and their origin and evaluate whether engaging in them is beneficial or harmful.

ASSESSING PAST TRAUMAS

Once therapists have assessed their client's current situation and ensured they are safe and stable, they can delve into past experiences. It can be difficult for clients to fully heal and move on without addressing these past traumas. Therefore, therapists must create a safe and supportive environment where clients can explore and process these experiences without feeling judged or invalidated.

PSYCHOEDUCATION

Psychoeducation is an essential early step in therapy for individuals who have experienced undue influence. One aspect of this is teaching clients about healthy coping mechanisms and strategies for managing the trauma they have experienced. Another critical part is educating them about the tactics of cults and other groups to exert control over their members.

A good foundation uses the Influence Continuum and the BITE Model, which both provide a framework for understanding mind control techniques. By having clients fill out a BITE Model for their respective groups, they can better understand the tactics used to influence and control them. This tool can be powerful for clients to recognize the extent of the influence that they are under and begin to take back control over their own lives. Scheflin's Social Influence Model (SIA) is another valuable tool to help your client understand the dynamic, interactional aspect of undue influence.

TEACHING ABOUT WHAT IS SAFE, NORMAL, AND HEALTHY

Many individuals involved in cults for an extended period may have a skewed perspective on what is normal and healthy. This could be due to the influence of the group's ideology, which can lead to a distorted view of reality. As a result, they may struggle with fundamental aspects of daily life, such as establishing healthy relationships or managing their emotions effectively. Therefore, it's vital to help clients understand the differences between a safe and a destructive organization and to provide them with the tools to establish a healthy baseline for their life outside of the cult.

WHAT DOES A HEALTHY CHILDHOOD LOOK LIKE?

In healthy, authoritative families, parents prioritize their children's needs and allow them to grow and develop their individuality, as opposed to authoritarian parenting, which focuses on obedience and control. Therefore, educating former cult members on what a healthy childhood looks like is essential, as well as providing examples such as playing, celebrating holidays, and questioning authority. By understanding the differences between authoritative and authoritarian parenting, they can learn to recognize unhealthy patterns and work towards healing.

HOME EDUCATION VS. PUBLIC EDUCATION

Former cult members may have been home-schooled or received a unique education that differs from traditional public schooling, such as a religious-based education focused on specific teachings and beliefs. Many destructive cults insist on schooling their children to keep them from the outside world, which they often consider to be evil or immoral.

The type of education a former cult member receives can have a significant impact on their worldview and ability to function in society. Exploring a client's educational experience can help identify any indoctrination or thought control techniques that may have been employed and work towards undoing any adverse effects that may have resulted.

EXPOSURE TO THE INTERNET AND SOCIAL MEDIA

Former cult members may have had limited or no internet or social media access during their time in the group. But conversely, they may have been recruited and indoctrinated online. Therefore, it's crucial to assess the former cult member's exposure to the internet and social media during their time in the group and provide education on media literacy to help them discern factual information from propaganda or disinformation. In addition, they should learn how to evaluate the safety of a website and become a critical consumer of social media rather than being controlled by it.

CHILD ABUSE

Former cult members often have a history of childhood abuse, either before their involvement in the group or during their time in the cult, if they were born and raised within it. Therefore, therapists must understand the various types of abuse that can occur, such as physical, verbal, emotional, sexual, and neglect. While it's necessary to address past traumas, it's equally important to focus on the present and assist clients in developing coping mechanisms and healthy behaviors to move forward.

ATTACHMENT STYLE

Attachment theory suggests that early life experiences with caregivers shape how we relate to others as adults—those who experienced insecure attachment in childhood may struggle with intimacy and relationships in adulthood. Likewise, individuals born and raised in a cult will have experienced disruptions in their attachment relationships due to their cult experiences. Therefore, therapists must create a safe therapeutic relationship where clients can explore and understand their attachment patterns, learn how to regulate their emotions and develop new, healthier ways of relating to others.

PARENTAL ALIENATION

Parental alienation occurs when children are turned against one parent by the other parent, and is a common issue when a parent leaves a cult. The parent who remains in the cult may believe their former spouse is evil for leaving the group and the family. Often, the parent tries to persuade their spouse to leave with them and keep the family together. Cult superiors will want to keep the children and parents "loyal." Therefore, they may believe they must indoctrinate the children against the other parent. Therapists need to learn whether their client has been impacted by parental alienation, either as a child or as a parent, and how it has impacted their relationships with family members. Understanding the Influence Continuum and BITE Model has proven vital to explain to children programmed to hate their parents. It helps them understand what happened to them so they can take the first steps toward reconciling with that parent.

CRITICAL THINKING, GUT FEELING, INNER VOICE

Developing critical thinking skills, listening to one's inner voice, and following gut feelings are essential for personal growth and decision-making. Therapists can educate clients that they have multiple aspects or parts of themselves and that by understanding and integrating these different parts, individuals can navigate their thoughts and emotions more effectively. Critical thinking is particularly valuable for former cult members as it can help them evaluate information and ideas presented by the group, allowing them to become more independent and empowered thinkers.

FOCUS ON THE PRESENT

Therapists can help clients develop skills to stay grounded in the current moment. It is essential that human beings understand that the past has already happened and the future hasn't happened yet. Therefore, being in one's body in the "now" becomes incredibly important. Dwelling on past mistakes or missed opportunities is not productive, and instead, therapy should focus on what they can do now. While the past may provide valuable information, it is crucial not to get stuck in traumatic memories, especially those related to their involvement in the cult. By prioritizing the here and now, clients can develop a sense of agency and control over their present circumstances, which is essential for their recovery.

Staying grounded in the present and on forming new memories allows individuals to regain control and focus on what they can do now, rather than being trapped by past trauma or regrets.

SOME ADDITIONAL CONSIDERATIONS

If both parents leave the group, it is their duty to keep their children safe and establish boundaries from the group, especially if they are very young.

When counseling a cult member, it's important not to use persuasion to argue or command the client to leave a group. Don't try to take the group or their beliefs away from them or to permanently and unilaterally pull them away from the group. This can lead the client to feel threatened and defensive, and rightly so. Instead, therapists can offer different perspectives and options for growth. By introducing new possibilities and helping individuals see choices they may not have considered, therapists can empower their clients to feel in control of the process and make the best decisions for themselves.

As we have seen, mind control does not completely erase a person's true self. Instead, it creates a dominant cult identity that suppresses the individual's authentic self. Cult indoctrination is akin to a mind control virus that can be cured. Once the virus is eradicated, the person's mental and emotional well-being can be restored, allowing their true self to resurface and integrate their cult experiences into a healthy framework.

It is my observation that when someone who has been unduly influenced is given a free choice and can overcome learned helplessness, they do not choose to stay enslaved — not when they could be making decisions for their own life, having normal relationships with other people, and pursuing their interests and dreams.

Many people view cult members as desiring a situation where they do not need to feel the pressure of thinking or acting for themselves. However, in my view people are naturally inclined towards growth and learning, so my approach focuses on education. As a therapist, I teach my clients about psychology, communication, mind control issues, and other destructive cults. I also provide much material about the specific cult they were involved in, including its history, leadership structure, and any doctrinal contradictions. Through this education, I aim to empower my clients with the knowledge to help them understand their experiences, make informed decisions, and ultimately move toward healing and recovery.

REFLECTIVE EXERCISES

1. What are some of the immediate needs that a client may have upon exiting a destructive cult?

_____

_____

_____

_____
_____
_____
_____
_____
_____
_____

2. Why is it essential to assess whether a former cult member is still involved in the practices or rituals of a cult after leaving?

_____
_____
_____
_____
_____
_____
_____
_____
_____

3. Think about a client you have worked with who may have experienced undue influence. What were some of the specific therapeutic considerations you had to address with them?

_____
_____
_____
_____
_____
_____
_____
_____
_____

4. Why is developing critical thinking skills essential in the recovery process for former cult members?

_____

_____

_____

_____

_____

_____

_____

_____

_____

_____

_____

CLINICAL QUALITIES

Working with former cult members can be challenging, and therapists must develop specific clinical qualities to provide the best possible care. These qualities apply not only to cult members but also to other patients.

CURIOSITY

A curious therapist approaches each client with an open mind and seeks to understand their unique story without preconceived notions or biases. It is essential to avoid fitting the client's story into a pre-existing framework, as this can result in missing important details and nuances. Instead, a curious therapist will ask questions and actively listen to the client's responses, gaining a deeper understanding of their experiences and needs.

EMPATHY

It is essential to have empathy and compassion for one's clients. Still, it is equally vital to avoid over-identification and maintain healthy boundaries to avoid becoming overwhelmed or traumatized by their experiences. One technique that can help therapists maintain these boundaries is creating a window outside their body. This technique involves listening to the client's story without letting it enter one's body directly, allowing the therapist to remain grounded and avoid experiencing the client's trauma.

ATTUNED LISTENING SKILLS

Attuned listening skills involve turning off one's internal dialogue and genuinely listening to the client, taking in information so well that it can be repeated to the client accurately. Therapists can help clients feel heard and understood by demonstrating active listening skills creating a safe space to explore their experiences and emotions.

HOPEFUL OUTLOOK

While it is essential to be optimistic, having realistic expectations about the therapeutic process is equally important. Clients may ask how long it will take to recover, and while there is no one-size-fits-all answer, therapists can offer guidance based on their experience. A critical period for transformative change is one year, but it can take longer, especially for those who have been in a cult for many years.

KNOWING WHEN TO SHARE PERSONAL INFORMATION

Therapists are usually taught to keep their personal stories out of the therapeutic relationship, and rightly so, but sharing personal experiences about having been in a cult can sometimes be beneficial in helping former cult members feel understood and less alone. By modeling vulnerability and normalizing the client's experiences, therapists can build a solid therapeutic relationship rooted in trust and understanding.

DISCRIMINATE FALSE VS. TRUE MEMORIES

Clients should be believed and taken seriously in therapy, and therapists should avoid dismissing any of their experiences. However, it is also important to approach the client's report of memories with discernment. There is a delicate balance between helping your clients feel safe and that they can trust you and communicating important factual information.

For example, if a client reports a memory of being one or two years old and in their crib and being molested with detail, one can say something like, "It sounds like you are pretty certain that this took place. Can you tell me when you had this memory surface, please?"

If they say something like when they were in the cult workshop or with a previous therapist who was using hypnosis, then you can reply with something like, "Very interesting" or "Very curious."

Many options exist depending on the rapport and trust established, including waiting for a future time to unpack this memory. Another option is to ask, "Are you curious to know if I have worked with other clients who reported similar beliefs but later realized they had been unduly influenced?"

There are numerous other therapeutic options therapeutically, including sharing that having clear memories at age one or two is not considered reliable.

Therapists can ask questions to understand the client's perspective and determine the accuracy of their memories. By allowing clients to connect the dots for themselves and also presenting information in a non-judgmental way, therapists can help clients come to their own conclusions about their experiences.

NON-JUDGMENT

Therapists must avoid being judgmental. Many therapists need to learn how to work with individuals who were perpetrators of horrendous psychological, physical, and even sexual abuse. Of course, mandatory reporting is required in many states regarding harm to children or criminal intentions and threats to harm. By focusing on the client's strengths and potential, therapists can create a safe space for clients to explore their experiences and emotions. When necessary, look for the injured child in that perpetrator or other parts of the client that you can focus on helping. The fact that they are in treatment means that a part wants relief from suffering.

REFLECTIVE EXERCISES

5. Reflect on a time when a client's story challenged your ability to remain non-judgmental. How did you handle this situation, and what strategies did you use to maintain an open and non-judgmental attitude?

_____

_____

_____

_____

_____

6. Has a client's experiences ever challenged your preconceived notions about them? How did you approach this situation, and what did you learn from it?

Individuals who have experienced authoritarian mind control have undergone distinct traumatic experiences that can result in severe emotional and psychological distress. As a result, there are specific therapeutic considerations that must be taken into account when working with this population. The primary focus for therapists must be to ensure the safety and well-being of their clients before helping them regain their autonomy and embark on the journey of healing and recovery. Additionally, employing clinical qualities such as empathy, active listening, and non-judgment is crucial in building a robust therapeutic relationship and providing compassionate care for individuals impacted by cult experiences.

MODULE 8 RESOURCES

Freedom of Mind Resources

Please use the search box on freedomofmind.com to search for resources.

Steven Hassan's dissertation: The BITE Model of Authoritarian Control: Undue Influence, Thought Reform, Brainwashing, Mind Control, Trafficking, and the Law

Websites

Dissociative Disorders expert, psychiatrist Marlene Steinberg' website.

Stranger in the Mirror: Dissociation—The Hidden Epidemic by Marlene Steinberg

Amy J.L. Baker, Parental Alienation Researcher, Expert, Author, Coach

Books

Tiny Habits: The Small Changes That Change Everything by BJ Fogg

The author presents a method for achieving personal transformation through the cultivation of small, manageable habits that lead to significant life changes.

Attachment Disturbances in Adults by Daniel P. Brown and David S. Elliott

This work offers an in-depth exploration of attachment theory and its application to treating relational and psychological issues in adults.

Feeling Good: The New Mood Therapy by David D. Burns

The book introduces cognitive behavioral techniques for combating depression, emphasizing the power of thought patterns in influencing mood and well-being.

MODULE 9: STRATEGIES & TECHNIQUES FOR WORKING WITH FORMER CULT MEMBERS

Summary: Provides therapists with strategies and techniques for aiding individuals recovering from cult involvement, covering various therapeutic interventions.

Learning Objectives: Equip mental health professionals with skills to address challenges faced by former cult members, focusing on empowering clients to reclaim control over their lives.

This module provides therapists with various strategies and techniques to aid individuals in recovering from cult involvement. By developing and utilizing a robust toolbox of methods, therapists can help clients establish balance and harmony between mind, body, and spirit and develop their inner potential. The goal is to empower individuals to control their own minds and bodies, and to teach them how to heal their wounds, discern ethical influences from unethical ones, identify healthy boundaries, and identify destructive predators to establish healthy relationships and live their authentic selves fully.

INSIGHTS FOR WORKING WITH THIS POPULATION

Understanding if the Client was Born or Raised in a Cult or Was Recruited Later

When someone is raised in a destructive group, they are often raised in authoritarianism, which often includes corporal punishment but always emphasizes obedience and not play and curiosity.

Unique Family Dynamics in Cults

Understand the distinct family dynamics for those born or raised in destructive groups. These dynamics are intrinsically linked to the cult experience and should be addressed accordingly. Many cults excommunicate or shun former members and try to pressure them to "repent" and rejoin. When people first leave, they might continue listening to cult propaganda or do cult rituals that will prolong their safe exit.

Clients often express frustration that clinicians do not understand their experiences within a cult and that extensive time is dedicated to educating the clinician about the nature of undue influence.

Understanding Loss and Mourning

Recognize that clients may be grieving the loss of their community and, in some cases, their family. This deep sense of loss is a critical aspect of their healing journey.

Individualized Recovery Approaches

Respect each client's unique path to recovery. Avoid imposing a standardized treatment method and be mindful that specific therapeutic tools might trigger trauma responses. For instance, DBT has a rule that can trigger former members because it mirrors "shunning" done in cults.

Not Blaming the Victim

Encourage a therapeutic approach that helps people realize they were deceived and manipulated. They didn't know what they didn't know about how destructive people and cults operate. Cults program members to always blame themselves for all problems.

Beyond Childhood & Personal Issues

A typical error is to jump to family-of-origin issues instead of focusing on the "here and now" and empowering their clients. Are they safe? Sleeping well? Eating, exercising? Do they have support? Emphasize that their involvement in a cult is not a reflection of unresolved childhood issues or personal deficiencies. Therapists should avoid over-focusing on family problems and instead address the trauma experienced within the cult.

Diverse Reasons for Cult Involvement

Acknowledge that there is no single 'type' of person who joins a cult. Clients come from various backgrounds and have different reasons for their involvement, which need to be understood on an individual basis. There are many intelligent, educated people from stable families who get caught up in destructive relationships and groups.

Believe and Respect Their Stories

It's crucial to listen without disbelief or judgment. The experiences shared may be shocking, but they were the client's reality. Shaming them for their actions within the group is hurtful and wrong. Likewise, many clients carry false beliefs and memories about their family, and immediately believing and validating stories about abuse can cause harm. Likewise, encouraging a client to disconnect from everyone in their past can be very bad advice.

Addressing Abuse as a Norm

Be aware that many clients may have experienced routine physical, sexual, and spiritual abuse. Recognizing this as a part of their past is vital in their healing process.

Facilitating an "Internal Locus of Control"

Rather than exerting your authority as an expert, encourage people to think for themselves. Encourage people to feel and express their feelings. Help them learn what is "normal" and "healthy." Never impose your beliefs, especially when it comes to religion. Assist clients to take time and learn and explore. Life is a journey, not a destination.

Creating a Safe Space for Healing

Above all, ensure that clients feel heard, understood, and safe. Help them recognize their uniqueness and interests. This foundation is essential for effective therapy.

THERAPEUTIC TOOLS

Therapists will be most effective if equipped with various tools to help clients heal and recover, regardless of their psychological challenges. Then, they can teach them how to control their own minds and not be controlled by emotions or beliefs that are hurtful or constricting. They can direct the person to develop confidence and trust in themselves, as well as in their ability to evaluate any future person or involvement. These tools benefit those who have experienced trauma throughout their lifetime.

ASSOCIATED VS. DISSOCIATED MEMORY

It is valuable to teach clients they can have a choice in how they relate to their memories. Understanding the difference between associated and dissociated memories is vital. Associated memories are those in which you relive the experience and feel like you are in the moment again. When experiencing associated memories, one feels the emotions and sensations connected with the memory as though you were back in the original experience. PTSD is one example. Something triggers the trauma, and the person gets revictimized again, in part bringing the past into the present.

I teach my clients that they can choose to recode memories, especially traumatic ones. One technique is teaching the client to stay grounded in their body and the safe present and then "recode" the past trauma by imagining themselves viewing it on a screen off the side. In this process, they are looking at it with a third-person perspective and not reliving it. The trauma happened to the person's younger self, not their present self. In contrast to associated memories, one is detached from the feelings and sensations of the memory.

Both types of memories can be helpful in different contexts. Associated memories are best for positive experiences, allowing you to relive and enjoy the moment again. In this way, they can help bring the happiness of the past into the present. However, for traumatic memories, it is best to use dissociated memories as the default to separate oneself from the experience and avoid being triggered by it. One has the choice to relive something traumatic if one chooses to do so. One possible setting to do this might be if one is an actor and the script demands the character one is playing to react as a trauma victim.

People who have experienced trauma commonly recall the past as though they are re-living the experience. Therapists must help them default to dissociated memories of traumatic events so they don't become retraumatized by the memory. As mentioned, reprogramming their minds to view the traumatic event as if they're watching it on a TV or computer screen helps them stay present in the here and now and avoid being triggered by the memory. Therapists can remind clients that the event happened to their younger self, not their present self, and that they are in a safe space. Indeed, they are just having a memory and don't need to reenter the traumatic moment. This approach benefits clients with PTSD who may be triggered by traumatic memories.

NARRATIVE THERAPEUTIC APPROACHES

Narrative therapy is a powerful approach to helping people recover from cult experiences. This approach involves encouraging clients to write their cult stories to gain insight into their experiences and process their emotions.

I advised former members to write out their cult story in my 1988 book *Combating Cult Mind Control*. Writing helps one to unpack one's memories and assemble memories in a coherent chronological form.

By telling their stories, people can gain control over their experiences and begin to understand what happened to them. Writing the story down can also help individuals stay present in the here and now, and it prevents the need to keep repeating the story repeatedly. Another benefit of narrative therapy is that it can help people reclaim their sense of agency and identity. Through creating writing and journaling, individuals can begin to separate themselves from the cult identity that may have been imposed on them. This can be an empowering process that helps clients move toward recovery and healing.

CREATE NEW SUPPORT SYSTEMS

Former cult members often need help to untangle or rebuild their social support systems. Upon leaving a cult, many individuals are cut off from family and friends who remain members, leading to isolation and lack of support. Therefore, clients often need help identifying and developing new sources of support and connection, whether through building new friendships, reconnecting with old ones, or seeking support groups.

I recommend therapists exercise caution when connecting people with other former cult members. Always prioritize the client's safety and well-being. While these connections can offer valuable support due to shared experiences, becoming involved with ex-members who have not yet processed their emotions and experiences can be detrimental. Instead, I suggest seeking out individuals or groups that are further along in their healing journey or have a positive and healthy outlook on their experiences. Ultimately, the goal is to help clients create new, healthy connections to support their ongoing healing.

TEACH PAYING ATTENTION TO ONE'S NEEDS FIRST

People who have experienced authoritarian mind control have been conditioned to prioritize the group's or the cult's needs above their own, leading to self-sacrifice and neglect of their own needs. Encouraging clients to recognize their value and self-worth while emphasizing the importance of self-care can help them achieve a healthier balance in their lives. One helpful analogy is airplane safety instructions, a situation in which passengers are told to put on their own oxygen masks before assisting others. By prioritizing their own needs and well-being rather than always putting others first, individuals can lead more fulfilling lives and become better equipped to support others.

REFLECTIVE EXERCISES

1. Recall a positive experience from your life and describe it as an associated memory. How did remembering it as an associated memory make you feel?

_____

_____

_____

_____

_____

_____

_____

_____

_____

_____

_____

2. Now, think of a problematic event from your life and describe it as a disassociated memory. In what ways would describing your challenging experience as a disassociated memory differ from recalling it as an associated memory?

_____

_____

_____

_____

_____

_____

_____

_____

_____

_____

3. How did creating a disassociated memory for a problematic event affect your emotional response to past trauma?

_____

_____

_____

_____

_____

_____

_____

_____

_____

4. How can you help ensure your clients default to dissociated memories when recalling traumatic events?

_____

_____

THERAPEUTIC TECHNIQUES

People who have been in a destructive cult group experience unique traumas that require specialized therapeutic techniques. For example, individuals may struggle with identity confusion, loss of autonomy, black-and-white thinking, perfectionism, and difficulty reintegrating into society. Therapists can draw from various methods to address their client's specific needs.

If they hear a client express something like "I don't know who I am", they can respond with a question that helps them understand their pre-cult identity.

One question could be: "Well, when do you feel the most you?"

After discussion of this question, the therapist could follow, later, with a question asking, "Who do you want to be?" Note that it is important to wait patiently after each question; it might take five full minutes or more.

As we covered previously, the most significant challenge for people who leave destructive cults is the disruption of their authentic identity. This is even more pronounced for those born and raised in a cult who struggle to understand who they are outside the confines of the controlling group.

If they say they don't know who they want to be, you can help them to explore their interests further. For instance, if they expressed an interest in stand-up comedy, you could ask about their favorite comedian and what they like about the person. Another helpful technique is to ask them who they admire most outside of the cult and what attributes they possess that they would like to embody, such as honesty, humility, empathy, intelligence, or kindness. By asking open-ended questions and giving individuals space to reflect, you can help them discover new aspects of themselves and identify their values and goals.

LIFE IS A JOURNEY; THERE IS NO "ONE" STATIC "YOU."

The model Freud put forth of id, ego, and superego has long been superseded by the realization that many parts of our psyche evolve over time. Many adults have blocks because, unconsciously, they are still using a script they learned as a young child. For example, a seven-year-old who is molested has very few resources for saying "no."

However, adults must be made aware that they can develop many options to avoid abuse or, if need be, escape, fight, yell, or physically defend themselves if necessary. People in cults are often taught that there is only one truth and one true "calling" for them. Clients often need help recognizing that they are multifaceted individuals with the capacity to change and grow. There is no "one" version of themselves. We change and grow all the time. Especially in this age of swift change, we must make sure to encourage flexibility, adaptability, and resilience in our clients.

Life is a process of uncovering interests, values, beliefs, and goals, which may evolve and change over time. Encouraging clients to explore different aspects of themselves and embrace the journey of self-discovery will help them shed the limiting beliefs and expectations imposed by the cult. This process can facilitate the emergence of a new sense of identity and purpose for the individual.

ORIENTATION TOWARDS LEARNING AND GROWTH VS. PERFECTIONISM

Cults often promote a culture of perfectionism. There is rigid, all-or-nothing, black-and-white thinking, and cult members are expected to adhere to strict rules and standards of behavior without question. Consequently, there is an accompanying sense of inadequacy and failure for someone who inevitably falls short of these impossible standards. To counteract this, therapists can help clients shift their orientation from perfectionism to a growth-oriented mindset. It's important to acknowledge that growth involves making mistakes and using those experiences as opportunities for learning. By adopting a growth mindset, individuals can let go of the pressure to be perfect and embrace the journey of self-discovery and healing. Unfortunately, too many people are raised with the ideology of perfectionism, and this is a huge reason so many people suffer needlessly, feeling that whatever they accomplish isn't perfect instead of looking at their accomplishments and acknowledging that no human being is perfect. In competitive sports, like gymnastics, there have been people like Simone Biles who can get a perfect score based on the criteria established by people in the sport. But it is critical to remember that even Simone Biles makes mistakes. In fact, she even experienced a mental health crisis and had to withdraw from several events during an Olympic competition.

PEOPLE HAVE FIVE OR MORE CAREERS THROUGHOUT THEIR LIFETIME

Destructive cults often impose the belief that one's job or purpose in life is predestined or must be approved by God, with any deviation seen as a failure to fulfill one's calling. Such a rigid mindset hinders individuals from realizing their full potential.

Research cited by Bruce Feiler in his book *Life is in the Transitions: Mastering Change at Any Age* shows that people nowadays typically switch careers five or more times in their lifetime, contrary to the traditional notion of sticking to one job for life. Therapists can emphasize to their clients that they have the freedom to explore different career paths and discover fulfillment in new areas. Encouraging an open-minded approach and investigating career options that align with their values and interests can help them find a renewed sense of purpose.

Disclosure: Feiler interviewed me for this book. Indeed, my involvement with the Moon cult altered my life trajectory.

FOCUS ON SKILLS AND STRATEGIES

Therapists can assist individuals in identifying and developing positive values such as humility, kindness, and honesty as they explore their interests, career options, and life goals. Additionally, therapists can encourage clients to build new networks of friends and contacts, as personal connections such as classmates, colleagues, and friends often lead to job opportunities and new careers. With the help of the internet, it's easier than ever to reconnect with people in their lives that they may have lost touch with during their time in the cult.

EVOLVE FROM SIMPLISTIC BINARY CHILDISH THINKING

Therapists can help individuals break free from the rigid, black-and-white thinking the cult may have instilled. This involves reprogramming their simplistic binary view of the world, in which everything is categorized as good or evil. Instead, therapists can help clients see the variation in ways of being and living, encouraging them to explore the nuances of life and embrace the gray areas. By doing so, clients can expand their understanding of the world and themselves, finding new meaning beyond the cult's limiting beliefs and expectations.

NEURODIVERSITY — START WITH STRENGTHS AND INTERESTS

When working with individuals on the autism spectrum, it's essential to recognize their qualities and strengths instead of trying to fit them into society's traditional modes. By focusing on their unique talents, therapists can help clients with autism develop a positive sense of self and identity. For example, if an individual is fascinated with trains, therapists can explore that interest and help them expand their knowledge and skills. In addition, listening carefully to their preferences often provides valuable clues to their strengths and potential growth areas. At times, they are not as constrained by the "noise" that neurotypicals must learn to overcome. They often have a profound ability to focus.

JAGGED PROFILE: NEURODIVERSITY INCLUDING ASD, ADHD, DYSLEXIA

A jagged profile refers to a pattern of strengths and weaknesses in a person's cognitive or behavioral functioning. It means an individual may excel in certain areas while struggling in others. It applies to individuals with what neurotypicals term "disabilities," such as ADHD, dyslexia, and ASD (autism spectrum disorder). Therapists should focus on building upon the person's strengths while addressing difficulty areas. By doing so, individuals can learn to see themselves positively and recognize their unique talents and skills. There is more than one way to measure intelligence or value.

INTENSIVE IN-PERSON SESSIONS

Traditional one-hour-a-week therapy is usually insufficient for working with someone born or raised in a cult or exiting a destructive relationship or group. The people who do best take their recovery seriously and are highly motivated and willing to read books, watch documentaries, and follow up on work suggested or assigned by the therapist. Writing down their story, as mentioned previously, is helpful if someone can do this. As is the case for most people, they have limited funds and may be juggling two jobs already just to pay rent and put food on the table.

Intensive in-person therapy sessions, which involve longer blocks of time, can be much more effective. Compared to the traditional model, which may take years to see results, intensive sessions can provide more focused and in-depth work, leading to quicker and more substantial progress. The case study mentioned earlier in the course—former Bible cult member, Laura—demonstrates what I believe is a widespread phenomenon of missed diagnosis and, therefore, improper treatment.

If someone is experiencing significant challenges, I have done intensive sessions over four days: Monday, Tuesday, Thursday, and Friday, with Wednesday off. The therapist can devote their full attention to the client with this model. This model of profound change work totals 24-30 hours of work in a week. However, I need to train more people willing to learn and do this work. At the time of writing this book, I am seventy years old and wish to pass on my knowledge to as many people as possible. I have five more books I wish to write.

Reflective exercises, relevant videos, or reading material can be assigned for the day off during intensive therapy sessions. Therapists may also suggest that a spouse or family member attend for some parts of the intensive week to understand and empathize with what the individual has experienced, which can improve the quality of their connection. However, while intensive sessions provide a focus and depth of work unparalleled by any other form of therapy, they may not be suitable for everyone, especially those who have difficulty sitting for long periods or concentrating.

While virtual meetings have become commonplace since the pandemic, many therapists do not believe they are not as effective as in-person sessions. There is a power to the healing relationship, and being in-person is a powerful way to help foster this relationship. The therapist can connect more deeply with the client and work towards achieving their goals.

IDENTIFYING AND UNDOING TRIGGERS

A trigger is an unconscious activation of a cue through one or more of the five senses. It could be something internal, like a thought or mental image, or external, like a person or place. For example, suppose you were in a cult where they played a specific song regularly during training sessions. Then, years later, if that same song comes on the radio, you may experience a negative trigger that mentally takes you back to the training program. Negative triggers stop someone from being present, and they revert to a point in the past when they were in the cult.

The first step in undoing a trigger is to become conscious that you have been triggered. This requires a certain level of self-awareness. The next step is to identify what triggered you. Once you have done that, next, reflect on how most people typically respond to that cue or stimulus. Then, you can deliberately pair the trigger with a new reaction you want, neutralizing the trigger. Finally, repeating the new response several times will help make it automatic.

For example, after I came out of the Moonies, I would think of Sun Myung Moon whenever I heard the word "moon." To undo the trigger, I would repeat the word *moon* repeatedly, visualize the moon, and say to myself, "The Earth has only one natural satellite, the moon." By reinforcing the actual meaning of the word *moon* rather than the cult connotation, I could neutralize and re-associate the trigger.

REFLECTIVE EXERCISES

5. Recall one of your triggers, such as a smell, taste, or sound, that provokes a mild adverse reaction. Follow the steps outlined above to neutralize the trigger. Reflect on your experience of this process and describe whether you successfully paired the trigger with a new, more positive reaction.

_____

_____

_____

_____

_____

_____

_____

_____

_____

_____

_____

_____

CAUTION ON GROUP THERAPY

Group therapy can be counterproductive and even dangerous for individuals in the early stages of their treatment. Being in a group setting where painful stories are shared can be undesirable for some individuals, especially those who have recently left a harmful cult. Additionally, they may be surrounded by others who are less functional than themselves, which can further exacerbate their distress. It's important to remember that individuals who have just left a cult are often cautious and skeptical about being in any group setting again. It may take time for them to feel comfortable enough to participate in a therapeutic group. It is important that the clients are informed of these possibilities, but to remind them that they are not bound to find these experiences traumatizing or even negative. On the contrary, many clients have benefited from these settings.

Although group therapy can be risky for individuals not yet far into their recovery process, there is enormous value in hearing stories from members of different cults. It can broaden one's perspective and challenge beliefs. For example, individuals from several other groups may think their leader was the Messiah. This helps people to challenge the idea that only their group taught the truth. So, if a client has progressed enough in their healing process, group therapy can be helpful. However, ensuring that it is appropriate and professionally led is essential. Dual relationships should be avoided, where a therapist sees clients individually while working with them in a group. It's also necessary to evaluate participants thoroughly to avoid hidden agendas or sabotaging behavior, for example, ensuring that an individual has not joined a new destructive group and is not using group therapy as an opportunity for recruitment.

During therapy sessions, the therapist must be vigilant about using cult terms, loaded language, and other potential triggers like songs or clothing. Former cult members who regularly associate with other former members can sometimes keep the cult's loaded language alive by using it when talking to one another. This practice is highly discouraged as it may impede progress.

Therapists must remain attentive during therapy sessions and notice if any participants get triggered. If this happens, they should address the issue and support the individual in working through it. While the goal is to empower individuals to think for themselves, therapists can be more direct initially and offer concrete suggestions as clients build confidence in their abilities. Sometimes, giving specific advice is the ethical choice to help empower someone in exiting a destructive situation.

CAUTIONS FOR THERAPEUTIC INTERVENTION

When providing therapeutic intervention to individuals who have been in cults, it is essential to exercise caution and consideration for their unique experiences and needs.

Here are some to keep in mind:

- Don't rush to recommend medication: While medication may be necessary sometimes, it should not be the default solution. Instead, exploring other therapeutic approaches and understanding the individual's situation is beneficial before considering medication. Of course, sometimes, a person needs something acutely, like getting some sleep. (I highly recommend reading this short book by radiologist and colleague Elvira Lang: Sedation without Medication: Rapid rapport and quick hypnotic techniques A Resource Guide for Doctors Nurses and Technologists)

- *Reevaluation of sleep:* Poor sleep is common for individuals in high-control groups. Therapists should help clients develop healthy sleep habits and address the root causes of any sleep issues. To learn more, hear my interview with sleep psychologist Lauren Broch. Also, consult a list of good practices here and the book by Matthew Walker, *Why We Sleep: Unlocking the Power of Sleep and Dreams*

- *Use of alcohol and other drugs:* Substance abuse can be a common coping mechanism for individuals in cults, so the therapist needs to explore whether this may be an issue.

- *Addiction screening and referral for treatment:* Therapists must be mindful of other potential addictions and refer their clients for specialized treatment if required.

- *Screen for suicide risk:* Therapists should be vigilant in screening for suicide risk among individuals who have left high-control groups. It's essential to have a plan to manage potential risks, such as referring them to suicide hotlines or emergency room. Follow-up questions can help determine the level of risk, such as asking if they have thought about how they would carry out the act. If the person has a specific plan, they may be at higher risk and require immediate attention.

- *Evaluate for personality disorders:* Former cult members can exhibit symptoms often misconstrued as being related to schizoaffective disorder, bipolar disorder, or personality disorders. However, therapists should consider the possibility that a client's symptoms and behaviors may result from a psychological disorder.

- *Developmental psychology considerations:* Many individuals in high-control groups may have missed out on developmental experiences, especially those born and raised in a cult. Therapists should be mindful of this and tailor their approach accordingly.

- *Adoption can be a complicating factor:* Therapists working with adoptees who have been in a cult should be aware of the additional trauma they may face and the unique challenges they may encounter.
Expert in this area, Dr. Joyce Maguire Pavao, suggests switching adoption from family-centered to child-centered, meaning that the focus should be on finding the right family for the child rather than the other way around.

- *Autism Spectrum Disorder:* Individuals who have been in high-control groups and are also on the autism spectrum may face unique challenges in therapy. These challenges can be addressed by developing specific strategies and accommodations that cater to their needs.

- *No significant life changes or commitment:* Clients should be encouraged to pace themselves in their recovery process lovingly and not rush ahead with major life decisions such as marriage or joining the military. However, therapists must respect their client's autonomy and freedom to make their own choices, even if they choose not to follow this advice.

THE POWER OF LANGUAGE

<u>Loaded language</u> can trigger an emotional response in those leaving a cult who have not learned about brainwashing and mind control. Even after leaving, cult words can cause anything from a flash of memory to a panic attack. Recovering from cult indoctrination includes examining one's vocabulary for loaded language and working towards freeing oneself of it. Using the right words can powerfully impact our thoughts and feelings. For this reason, I suggest that individuals seek therapy in their native language, especially if they were indoctrinated into a cult in another language.

Language shapes how we think and feel, and cults exploit this by using loaded words to control members.

Even with good intentions, clinicians, doctors, and family members can unintentionally trigger and undermine a person's recovery through the words they use. For example, saying, "I don't want you to think I'm pressuring you," can cause the client to feel pressured. Instead, it's essential to use words that promote feelings of safety and security, such as asking, "What steps can you take to ensure your safety?" or "Do you have someone to call if you need to talk?" Additionally, therapists must be cautious about using loaded terms and avoid using words associated with a particular cult until later in therapy, when triggers have been addressed.

Part of recovery is reclaiming the power and beauty of language. When someone is in a cult or abusive situation, their language is limited and controlled. Loaded words and clichés are used to manipulate thoughts and actions. Expanding their vocabulary and exploring different ways of expressing themselves is beneficial as they recover. Language should not limit but allow a range of emotions and experiences to be expressed. Reclaiming the robustness of language can be empowering and help individuals in their healing journey. It will enable them to communicate more effectively, express themselves authentically, and connect with others more profoundly.

Recognizing the use of loaded language is crucial for the recovery process, and having support from family, friends, and other members can be immensely helpful. As part of my Strategic Interactive Approach (SIA), I teach family members how to communicate effectively with their loved ones, emphasizing the importance of avoiding certain words that may trigger their family member's cult identity.

Former cult members should be guided to reclaim the ordinary meaning of words that have been imbued with specific connotations within the cult. For instance, in Scientology, the word "clear" has a distinct meaning that ex-members need to unlearn by pairing the word with its ordinary definition, as explained in the section on undoing triggers. In addition, loaded language essentially rewires the brain to internalize the cult's ideology, so reverting to everyday language can help speed up recovery.

Encourage clients to let go of guilt and shame when slip-ups occur and to see them as an opportunity to retrain the mind. It's a step-by-step process, but with persistence and patience, anyone can rid themselves of the lingering effects of cult influence and gain freedom of mind. It can be helpful to think of the recovery process as cleaning out the cobwebs from the past, as each step forward clears away some of the mental clutter and allows for clearer thinking and a more authentic sense of self.

REFLECTIVE EXERCISES

6. Consider recent times when you unintentionally used loaded language with a client or someone you know. How did you become aware of it, and how did it impact the client? Your reaction?

_____

_____

_____

_____

_____

_____

_____

_____

_____

7. Take some time to research the loaded language used by cults (watch videos, listen to podcasts, read members' experiences). List some of the terms you have learned about and what they mean in the cult.

For example, Scientology has an extensive dictionary of loaded language, and members are taught what is known as "study tech," which instructs them to look up cult word meanings at any moment of confusion or disagreement. This form of self-indoctrination is powerful and a significant issue facing many ex-Scientologists in therapy.

_____

_____

_____

_____

_____

HEALING GOALS

This component explores various healing goals for individuals who have left high-control groups. These strategies can empower individuals to take control of their own healing process and move forward with newfound insight and confidence.

CULTIVATING AN INTERNAL LOCUS OF CONTROL

People leaving an authoritarian relationship or group usually have trouble at first trusting their own decisions and often look to authority figures to tell them what to do. Having an internal locus of control is crucial for healing and empowerment. It means that individuals can take charge of their thoughts and actions rather than looking outside themselves to some authority figure to tell them what to do or what to believe. Therapists must be sensitive to this distinction and empower clients to take control of their minds and bodies. While providing guidance and suggestions, ultimately, the client needs to be encouraged to take charge of their healing process and decide what steps to take.

BEING IN THE "HERE AND NOW"

Help clients to stay grounded in the present moment and not get stuck dwelling on the past or consumed by anxiety about the future. Another vital idea is teaching clients to do a mental inventory to help make decisions: is an issue within or outside their own control?

I often spread my arms out to emphasize the importance of focusing on what's within one's control and letting go of what's outside of it. When clients have persistent thoughts outside their control, I may recommend compartmentalization or scheduling "worry time." This technique involves setting aside specific periods for worrying, three minutes, five times a day, to prevent negative thoughts from intruding during the rest of the day. This strategy changes the person's relationship with the problem, helps compartmentalize the worry, and frees up more time for productive behaviors.

TOOLBOX OF STRATEGIES AND TECHNIQUES FOR REALITY-TESTING

Having a toolbox of strategies and techniques for reality-testing is essential when working with individuals who have been involved in a cult. One such method is to ask specific questions that challenge their beliefs. For instance, a therapist can ask a client, "Has anyone ever referred to your group as a cult?" and follow up with questions such as, "Why do people say that?" or "Can you give specific examples of why they say your group is a cult?" By asking such questions, therapists can gain insight into the group's beliefs, behaviors, and practices and help the individual better understand their experiences. In addition, therapists can work with clients to fact-check information, seek multiple perspectives, and examine personal biases. With a well-rounded toolbox of strategies and techniques, individuals can learn how to effectively navigate the complexities of their past experiences and make informed decisions moving forward.

DECISION-MAKING STRATEGIES

Individuals who have left high-control groups may struggle with decision-making and often rely on others to choose for them. This is because destructive cults prioritize obedience and conformity over individual autonomy. Additionally, ex-cult members may struggle with perfectionism, as they have been conditioned to believe that mistakes are unacceptable and must strive for an unattainable level of perfection. As a result, decision-making can become paralyzing, as any potential mistake or misstep may feel catastrophic. Therapists can help their clients recognize that being human means we are not perfect, and striving for perfectionism can lead to unnecessary stress and anxiety. Instead, it is better to aim for aspirational effort, which means setting realistic goals and not devoting excessive time and energy trying to perfect something when they can achieve good results with a more reasonable effort.

TRUSTING ONESELF AND EVALUATING WHEN TO TRUST OTHERS

Developing the ability to trust oneself and evaluating whether to trust or mistrust others is a crucial part of the recovery process for former cult members. Therapists can guide clients to assess people's behavior more carefully by asking questions such as, "Are they kind to the elderly?" or "Do they lose their temper easily?" Additionally, clients should be encouraged to consider how others make them feel. For instance, do they feel pressured to join something immediately or fear missing out on something great?

Clients should be cautious of immediate friendships with strangers. Clients can be taught to visualize different circles emanating from their bodies, representing different levels of closeness with others. New people should be on the outer periphery until trust is established. Real friendships take time and involve shared experiences. Spending time with people who accept you for who you are and don't try to change you is best. Reciprocity is also critical in building trust and healthy relationships. By evaluating behavior and focusing on feelings and instincts, clients can learn to make more informed decisions about whom to trust and build strong, supportive relationships.

REFLECT ON THE KNOWLEDGE THEY HAVE NOW THAT THEY DIDN'T HAVE BEFORE

A powerful technique is to encourage clients to reflect on their past experiences and the knowledge and information they have now that they didn't have in the past. Therapists could guide clients to revisit critical moments, such as when they were recruited or their earliest memories of the cult, and ask them to imagine what they would have said or done differently if they had the knowledge they have now. By doing so, clients can gain a sense of empowerment and control over their thoughts and actions while healing their younger selves.

It's important to acknowledge that they did their best at the time with the knowledge and resources they had and that they have now grown and gained a new understanding. This technique can provide clients with the tools and skills to navigate similar situations in the future as they learn to trust themselves and their instincts. Ultimately, the goal is to help clients move forward with newfound insight and confidence.

EDUCATION ON NEUROPLASTICITY AND NEUROGENESIS

By educating clients about neuroplasticity and neurogenesis, therapists can help them realize that their past experiences do not have to define their present and future. Norman Doidge, a psychoanalyst and author of _The Brain That Changes Itself: Stories of Personal Triumph from the Frontiers of Brain Science,_ has presented many case studies and research findings that show how the brain can adapt and reorganize itself based on new experiences and activities. Understanding that the brain is malleable and can be rewired can give clients hope that they can heal and recover from cult indoctrination and programming.

SPIRITUALITY — WHAT IS THE PURPOSE OF LIFE?

Spirituality is an essential component of healing for ex-cult members, as it allows individuals to explore the purpose of life and find meaning beyond the limitations of their previous cult beliefs.

Individuals must explore and discover their own purpose. This journey of exploration may involve researching different religions and looking for healthy expressions of whatever religion they may be interested in, as well as exploring other spiritual practices such as prayer and meditation. It also includes considering a reconnection to ancestral spirituality or childhood religion. Learning about one's ancestral roots can provide insight into one's spirituality and help to heal the wounds of past trauma. Toxic beliefs such as nihilism, magical thinking, or the idea that Armageddon is imminent can lead to destructive behavior.

I frequently caution against institutions that claim their way is the only way, as this can lead to dogmatic thinking and limit personal growth. Instead, to challenge toxic ideologies, I encourage clients to focus on positive actions that benefit themselves, their community, and the world and to find a healthy community where they feel supported and valued.

Self-love and acceptance are fundamental principles of spirituality that can help individuals become more compassionate, kind, and positive forces in the world. Self-love should not be confused with egotism or narcissism, which is self-centered and lacks empathy for others. Every person has inherent value and deserves respect and dignity. By prioritizing love, acceptance, and contributing to the world, individuals can experience a sense of purpose and fulfillment.

POST-TRAUMATIC STRESS DISORDER (PTSD)

Post-traumatic stress disorder (PTSD) is a mental health condition that develops in some individuals who have experienced a traumatic event. While it is normal to feel fear during and after a traumatic situation, individuals with PTSD experience a range of common after-effects. According to Benjamin Colodzin, author of *How to Survive Trauma: A Program for War Veterans and Survivors of Rape, Assault, Abuse, or Environmental Disasters,* symptoms include vigilance and scanning, elevated startle response, blunted affect or psychic numbing, aggressive or controlling behavior, depression, anxiety, episodes of rage, substance abuse, intrusive recall, dissociative "flashback" experiences, insomnia, suicidal ideation, and survivor's guilt. For therapists working with individuals who are struggling with PTSD, it is essential to teach them how to neutralize their triggers and to be present in the moment.

While PTSD can be debilitating, traumatic events do not necessarily cause PTSD. It is my experience that if people are taught to be in the present, and in their body, they can be taught how to avoid retraumatization. However, by educating the client about it and its associated symptoms, therapists can help individuals recognize when they may be struggling and provide them with the tools and resources they need to manage and overcome it.

THE ROLE OF FAMILY AND FRIENDS

Family and friends play a crucial role in identifying signs of mind control or radicalization in their loved ones. Sudden changes in behavior, such as secrecy, unusual spending patterns, a drastic shift in beliefs, or the use of buzzwords and loaded language, can indicate that the individual is in a destructive group. Being sensitive and non-judgmental when approaching a loved one experiencing these changes is essential. Instead of attacking or accusing them of being involved in a cult or radical group, it is better to be curious and ask questions. By showing genuine interest and concern, family and friends can potentially help their loved ones avoid falling into the trap of mind control or radicalization.

When you realize someone you care about is involved with a potentially harmful group, it's essential to do your research and seek out former members or other experts for guidance. Family members can play a role in helping their loved ones by encouraging them to practice critical thinking and reality testing.

Adam Grant's book *Think Again: The Power of Knowing What You Don't Know* offers valuable advice for approaching beliefs with an open mind and a scientific mindset. By disconnecting one's ego from one's views and pursuing evidence-based information, individuals can assess the situation objectively and make informed decisions. Being willing to change one's mind shows strength in learning and adapting to new information.

Preparing for interacting with a family member involved in a cult can be challenging and emotionally taxing. However, rehearsing can help alleviate anxiety and improve communication. By visualizing different scenarios and anticipating the loved one's responses, family members can be better equipped to approach the conversation in a goal-oriented fashion. Practicing different responses to the best, worst, and most likely scenarios can provide a range of choices and eliminate the unknowns that create fear and anxiety. The more family members rehearse, the more comfortable they will become in constructively influencing their loved ones and potentially helping them leave the harmful group.

STRATEGIC INTERACTIVE APPROACH (SIA)

The Strategic Interactive Approach is a complex system approach creating a network of trained individuals (family, friends, ex-members, media, clergy, therapists) to orchestrate a step-by-step ethical influence program to empower an individual or set of individuals to think for themselves. It is directed towards asking questions in a warm, friendly, curious way that provokes the person to think differently or to do more research.

Since the public became more aware of destructive cults in the late 1960s, families have sought ways to rescue their loved ones. Early methods, such as deprogramming, were crude and sometimes illegal. Over the past three decades, counseling techniques, social psychology research, and the development of the Internet have provided us with more effective tools to break the chains. In previous approaches, family members were excluded from the process. Former cult members and deprogrammers would be in the same room as the cult member, but the family was not instructed on how to behave or informed of what was happening. To address this, I developed a new approach that involves family and friends. This approach invests time and effort in teaching them first and introducing them to former members before planning interventions. In the long run, empowering family and friends to be the influence is more effective. It is crucial to introduce the expert at the right moment when the person feels loved and supported and has the choice to discuss important issues.

The SIA offers a recovery process that addresses the long-term impacts of cult involvement on the member and their family. When someone joins a cult, it affects the entire family system. Parents may experience overwhelming emotions of guilt, fear, anger, and frustration. Long-standing marriages may be strained under the weight of the situation. Siblings may feel pressured to join the cult and labeled as evil if they refuse, causing frustration and anger towards the cult member. Pre-existing issues such as jealousy, mistrust, control, communication problems, and lack of intimacy can compound the situation and make navigating it even more challenging. The SIA aims to address these issues and provide a comprehensive recovery process for all those affected.

HYPOTHETICAL QUESTIONS

As part of the Strategic Interaction Approach, individuals are encouraged to consider essential questions that empower them to think critically and evaluate their situation. Through this process, individuals learn to rely on their inner voice and exercise their free will rather than being controlled by an authority figure. For example, to help individuals in cults consider leaving, hypothetical questions can be used in a non-judgmental and supportive environment. Individuals can explore their beliefs and experiences without feeling condemned or pressured by approaching the questioning process with curiosity and an open mind.

Here are some of the hypothetical questions I have used and found effective, as well as some commentary on each.

"WHAT IF GOD WANTS YOU TO LEAVE?"

When a person tells me they joined a cult because they had a spiritual experience and were guided by God, I acknowledge their experience without dismissing it. However, I use it as a clue to help them question their beliefs. I may ask a hypothetical question such as, "What if God came to you tonight and told you to leave this group? What would you do?"

Therapeutic hypothetical questions can encourage critical thinking and self-reflection, empowering individuals to explore their beliefs in a safe, open-minded space without fear of judgment.

Usually, a cult member initially denies this possibility, claiming that God would never ask them to leave. But by continuing to question and probe, they may eventually admit they would go if they knew it was God's will. I reinforce this by saying, "So, your commitment to God is more important to you than the group. Is that right?" They will often confirm this to be the case. This questioning technique helps them to re-evaluate their beliefs and priorities in a non-confrontational way.

"WHAT IF THE LEADER ADMITS HE IS NOT THE MESSIAH (PROPHET, APOSTLE, AVATAR, ENLIGHTENED MASTER)?"

When working with former members of the Moonies, I would ask them, "What if Father (Sun Myung Moon) gave a speech and admitted to seeing a therapist, being given medication, and realizing he's not the Messiah? What would you do?" Although they may initially respond with disbelief, this question can plant a seed of doubt and open up the possibility of leaving the group. Another question is, "What would need to happen for you to leave the group?" An example could be something like the leadership would have to commit a crime, or be found lying. By encouraging individuals to think critically and consider their own internal compass, they can begin to develop an understanding of when it may be time to leave the group. These answers can also be used to demonstrate that these "time to leave" criteria have already been met as these specific events may have already taken place inside the group and have been hidden from the member (see: Information Control in the BITE Model).

"WOULD YOU KILL YOURSELF (OR SOMEONE ELSE) IF THE LEADER ASKED YOU TO?"

While some of the hypothetical questions may be challenging, they encourage individuals to question their beliefs. For instance, one such question might ask what someone would do if asked to drink cyanide-laced flavor aid, like Jim Jones' followers. They might immediately say that would never happen, but I would press on and ask what they would do if it did happen. Would they leave or obey? I would then share the story of Dick Joslyn, a former client of mine who was a member of Heaven's Gate for 15 years and the number three person in charge of the group. He left five years before they killed themselves. When I asked him what caused him to leave, he said that he had promised himself when he joined the group that he would leave if they ever started talking about killing themselves. When they did start talking about it, he kept his promise and left, ultimately saving his life. I congratulated him on creating a line in the sand and honoring his commitment to himself.

"WHAT IF YOU DON'T EARN THE MONEY THE RECRUITER PROMISED?"

I use a similar approach with individuals who have joined multi-level marketing schemes, where they believe they can become millionaires by working part-time. First, I encourage them to set a specific financial goal for themselves, such as how much money they aim to make within the next three to six months. Then, I advise them to track their time and expenses. If they don't achieve that financial goal within six months or a year, they should promise themselves to leave, regardless of any rationalization, justification, or manipulation from the MLM. This strategy can effectively empower individuals to make their own decisions and not be swayed by the group's rhetoric. I don't tell people to leave or argue with them about the legitimacy of the MLM; instead, I help them establish clear goals and boundaries for themselves.

STRATEGIES FOR HEALING

These strategies can assist individuals who have experienced cult involvement to regain their authentic selves and move forward in their recovery journey.

- *Live in your body:* Encourage clients to be present in their bodies, paying attention to their feelings and physical sensations.

- *Live in the present*: Keep the client anchored in the current moment and not drifting back to the past or with preoccupations about the future.

- *Locus of control:* Foster an internal locus of control by empowering clients to rely on their inner guidance, not external sources, to tell them what to believe, feel, or do.

- *Emotions are our "friends":* Help clients view emotions as valuable sources of information and provide techniques to prevent them from becoming overwhelmed by their emotions.

- *Learning and growing:* Emphasize a growth model over success/failure or perfectionism.

- *Focus on goals:* Help clients identify their goals and focus on the actions that will bring them closer to achieving them, such as developing necessary skill sets.

- *Open-ended questions:* Use open-ended rather than directive questions to explore clients' thoughts and feelings.

- *Authentic vs. cult identity:* Be aware of whether your client responds as their authentic self or from their cult identity.

- *Normalizing questions and disagreement:* Help clients to feel safe challenging you and normalize questioning and disagreement.

- *Neurogenesis and neuroplasticity:* Educate clients about neurogenesis and neuroplasticity to help them understand that they can rewire their brains.

- *The therapeutic relationship:* Prioritize building a trusting relationship with clients and ask them what their goals are for therapy and what support they need from you to feel safe.

- *Extract positive experiences:* Encourage clients to recognize any positive experiences they had while in the cult, such as developing valuable skills like public speaking. Then, help them find ways to apply these skills in their current life.

- *Be your own friend:* Help individuals who have lost track of what is real and what is not by empowering them to figure it out. Encourage them to be a good friend to themselves and treat themselves kindly and compassionately. Ask them what advice they would give to their best friend in a similar situation and then apply it to themselves so they support themselves through recovery.

- *Normalize the inability to trust themselves:* Cults program members to believe that trusting themselves is selfish, making it challenging for individuals to trust their instincts. Additionally, many wonder how they can trust themselves again after they are recruited into a cult. It is important to normalize this struggle and help clients understand that learning to trust themselves is a journey. By teaching them about mind control, the Influence Continuum, and the BITE Model, clients can gain tools to evaluate individuals and groups in the future and make informed decisions.

- *Prioritize Safety:* Clients cannot heal until they are in a relatively safe environment. Therefore, help the client assess their level of safety and help them put a plan in place to achieve this so that they can begin to create a healthy sense of self.

This therapeutic work aims to help individuals restore their authentic selves by providing them with a toolbox of healing techniques and strategies. By undoing phobia programming, neutralizing triggers, and sorting through positive and negative experiences, clients can process their past cult involvement and become stronger. Empowering clients with education and tools enables them to liberate their cult self from the programming and move towards a more authentic and fulfilling life.

THREE-STEP PHOBIA CURE

Phobia indoctrination is the most powerful tactic for keeping cult members dependent and obedient. Individuals may stop believing in the leader and the doctrine but are still unable to walk away. Why? Because they are psychologically paralyzed with indoctrinated fears.

The three-step phobia intervention is an effective way to unlock cult phobias. Unfounded fears are stripped of their power and seen for what they are—proof of the group's banal destructiveness. In my experience, almost all cases of phobia are cured through visualization, suggestion, and experience. Most of the time, this method takes surprisingly little time. The three-step phobia intervention can be summarized as follows:

STEP ONE: PHOBIA VS. LEGITIMATE FEAR

Step one is explaining to the cult member the difference between a legitimate fear and a phobia. Explain that an irrational fear robs us of our power of choice. Freedom of mind means not letting emotions and negative thoughts or habits control us. Using examples of different phobias, you may also explain how a cure is possible.

I have found it helpful to prompt individuals with the question, "What if your worst fear came true?" Getting people to articulate their fears helps drain phobias of their power. For example, individuals who fear public speaking may worry that their audience will become disinterested or critical. However, once they verbalize these fears, they often see that the outcomes are not as catastrophic as imagined. Even if they deliver their worst speech, they will survive and may emerge from the experience stronger.

STEP TWO: EXPLAINING HOW OTHER GROUPS USE PHOBIAS

In step two, you discuss how other harmful groups or individuals intentionally instill phobias to manipulate people. First, you provide various examples of phobias cultivated by other groups and ask about the cult member's opinions of these groups. For example, you might talk about how some Jehovah's Witnesses would rather die than get a blood transfusion. Next, you highlight how individuals who have left these groups could recognize the presence of phobia indoctrination and use the cure to overcome their fears. By indirectly alluding to similar scenarios, you can educate the person about phobias without provoking an adverse reaction. Finally, you can explain how individuals who left other groups did not experience the catastrophic outcomes they feared while still in the group, demonstrating that these fears were unwarranted and implanted in the cult member by the group's manipulation.

STEP THREE: DISCUSSING SPECIFICS OF THEIR SITUATION

The last step aims for the individual to draw parallels between their group and the other cults that have been discussed. Again, the intention is for the individual to understand that their group, like the other cults, is manipulating its members. So, in step three, you delve into the particulars of their group or relationship. Once the individual understands the Influence Continuum and BITE Model and recognizes their situation, much of the influence on them will dissipate. For some, it feels like a bubble bursting. In 1976, my deprogramming ended when I had the experience that I liken to someone opening the curtains in a dark room. Sunlight came streaming in. I looked out the window, and I saw the greenery outside.

Start by asking the cult member if they have considered whether their group engages in similar behavior to other groups. Allow a moment of silence to let the question sink in.

Typically, the member will ask for clarification, which provides an opportunity to ask whether it's possible to leave the group and lead a fulfilling life. If the group is religious, inquire whether the member believes it's possible to leave and still have a connection with God.

Asking someone what they would be doing if they were happy with their life and the group never existed is a powerful question that can help bring out their authentic self. However, suppose the person cannot come up with a positive answer. In that case, a more indirect question can be asked, such as whether they believe it is possible for people outside the group to be happy and satisfied with their lives and what kinds of things those people might be doing. These questions encourage people to express themselves authentically and can profoundly impact their thinking.

REFLECTIVE EXERCISES

8. List some fears associated with cults that you could mention to your client in step two of the Phobia Cure (you may need to do some research.)

_____

_____

_____

_____

_____

_____

_____

_____

_____

_____

_____

_____

9. How do you balance the need to respect a client's beliefs and help them overcome phobias?

_____

_____

_____

_____

_____

_____

_____

_____

_____

_____

_____

_____

_____

_____

_____

_____

_____

_____

PEOPLE ARE BORN WITH AN AUTHENTIC SELF

An essential part of healing from authoritarian mind control is connecting with one's authentic self. As much as cult indoctrination attempts to suppress and destroy the authentic identity, it never wholly succeeds. There are too many experiences and too many positive memories that cannot be erased. The cult tries to bury these reference points and submerge the person's past. Yet, over time, the authentic self strives to resurface and regain its freedom.

Claire Frederick, MD was a psychiatrist well-known for her work in psychology, specifically in hypnotherapy and trauma treatment. She developed a therapeutic approach called the "center core phenomena," which focused on accessing individuals' inner resources and wisdom to help them heal from past traumas and achieve personal growth. Her approach was based on the belief that every person has innate qualities that can be accessed through hypnosis and other techniques.

The concept of center core phenomena involves tapping into one's inner wisdom and identifying resource states within oneself. This includes connecting with one's conscience, inner creativity, need for love, truth, and meaning, and connection with others. By doing so, individuals can create resource parts that act as protectors during uncertainty or fear. The idea is to trust oneself and develop an inner guide aligned with one's goals and values. Frederick's approach emphasizes the importance of connecting with oneself and developing a strong sense of inner strength and hope for a positive future.

What I found so illuminating was the encouragement to imagine parts of a person's psyche with specific strengths. For example, a part that is a protector or security guard. Here, there is a protector part. Also, a Wise part can be male, female, or a fictional character, like Merlin from the Arthurian legends. A creative part that can be called on to generate new ideas and solutions to problems. In fact, all internal resource parts can be anything or person, real or fictional.

APPROACHES FOR INTERACTION

Approaching someone about their involvement in a cult is a delicate process. It is essential to find a way to broach the topic without triggering their cult identity and provoking a negative, close-minded reaction. One practical approach is to ask indirect questions, encouraging the person to explore their experiences and beliefs. Additionally, asking about critical experiences that were pivotal to their commitment to the group or moments of doubt when they questioned their involvement can help the person recognize the manipulative tactics used by the group.

APPROACH THEIR CULT INVOLVEMENT INDIRECTLY

Avoid overtly criticizing the leader, doctrine, or policy, especially at the beginning of work with a client. Instead, follow their lead. Let them criticize, and you can validate and then bring up what they said to them if later they are defending the leader or the group. Approaching a client's cult involvement indirectly usually will be a more effective way to gain insight into their experiences.

Instead of directly telling them they were in a cult, therapists can ask if they have watched anything about cults or if they can identify any groups they see as cults. From there, therapists can do some psychoeducation, explaining the BITE Model and Influence Continuum and asking how they think their experience differs from those they see as cults. It's important to ask questions respectfully and without judgment, allowing the client to do the work and take their time in answering.

ASK ABOUT KEY EXPERIENCES PIVOTAL TO THEIR COMMITMENT

Asking about the key experiences pivotal to their commitment to the group can be a powerful tool. Through gentle questioning, therapists can identify the factors that contributed to their involvement and commitment to the group, for example, whether it was a spiritual experience, falling in love with the recruiter, or believing that the leader was the most brilliant person on earth. By examining these experiences more closely, therapists can help clients see how they were manipulated and deceived by the group and its leaders.

ASK THEM TO DESCRIBE MOMENTS OF DOUBT

Ask your client to describe the moments when they had doubts or questioned their involvement with the group. For example, suppose they have been a member for a long time. In that case, they may have experienced multiple instances where they considered leaving, such as feeling disillusioned, tired, or missing their family. Encourage them to explore these moments and identify the part of themselves that they wanted to leave. Did their experience with the group actually change, and was it ultimately a good decision to stay or return to the group? Keep in mind the question, "If you knew then what you know now, what would you do differently?" The ultimate goal is to help the individual reconnect with their true self.

CONNECT THE PERSON BACK TO THEIR AUTHENTIC SELF

Connecting a person back to their authentic self is vital in helping them regain their sense of identity after their cult involvement. One effective approach is asking the person how they envision a happy life without the group. By asking, "If the group never existed, and you were happy with your life, what do you think you would be doing?" you can encourage the person to explore their authentic desires and interests. Initially, the person may struggle to answer this question, but with time and persistence, they can envision a fulfilling and meaningful future.

EXPRESSIVE THERAPIES

Expressive therapies can be an effective tool to help them recover from the trauma they experienced. Expressive therapies such as art therapy, music therapy, play therapy, narrative therapy, movement therapy, psychodrama, animal therapy (such as equine therapy), and somatic therapy (such as massage and dance) can provide a safe and creative outlet for clients to explore their emotions and experiences. For example, massage therapy, which helps people get in touch with their bodies, could be therapeutic for people taught by a cult to deny their feelings or have had out-of-body experiences. In the hands of a skilled practitioner, patients would pay attention to what their body is feeling, become aware of areas of tension, and learn to relax. Secular meditation techniques can also be helpful in calming anxieties and bringing focus.

Expressive therapies provide non-verbal means for expressing emotion and may be effective for releasing painful memories. Through these therapies, clients can gain greater self-awareness and self-expression and learn new coping skills to deal with their past experiences. Therapists may assess which expressive therapy will be most beneficial for each client and incorporate them into the treatment plan.

COMMON AUTISM SPECTRUM DISORDER (ASD) CHALLENGES THAT MAY BE EXPLOITED

Individuals with Autism Spectrum Disorder (ASD) may be hypersensitive or hyposensitive to physical stimuli and may struggle with social interactions and understanding subtle messages. They may also exhibit repetitive, stereotyped, restricted, or compulsive behaviors and show inflexible thinking. These characteristics make them more vulnerable to cult recruitment and exploitation. The executive functioning of individuals with ASD is affected, impacting decision-making, regulating emotions and attention, and avoiding acting on impulses. They often prefer clear expectations, black-and-white thinking, direct communication, and regular routines.

Due to the lack of a robust theory of mind in individuals with ASD, they may have difficulty identifying that a group may have a hidden agenda. They may also feel isolated and lack an understanding of social pragmatics, leading to a limited network of friends. The preference for online interactions and gaming can lead to individuals being easily tricked, radicalized, and recruited into a cult by individuals who do not have their best interests at heart.

Cults' explicit, rigid rules and structure can appeal to individuals with ASD. Cults also provide a ready social group of people who "love bomb" them with positive attention. This can cause families of individuals with ASD to become less skeptical of a new group because they are happy that their loved one appears to have made lots of friends.

However, it is crucial to educate individuals with ASD about the tactics of cults and how to identify a group's hidden agenda to prevent exploitation. Using models such as the Influence Continuum and BITE Model can help them understand the tactics of manipulation and control used by cults. It is also essential to support them in developing self-advocacy skills, regulating their emotions, and impulse control.

REFLECTIVE EXERCISES

10. Take a moment to reflect on what you have learned in this course. How has your understanding of cult mind control evolved? What insights or new skills have you gained? What goals do you have for further development in this area?

_____

_____

_____

_____

_____

_____

_____

_____

STEVEN HASSAN'S BOOKS

Now that you have completed the Foundational Course for Clinicians, I highly recommend reading my books to go deeper into understanding mind control. To start, I suggest picking up the updated edition of _Combating Cult Mind Control_. Then, if you are interested in learning how to help people exit cults, the second one to read would be _Freedom of Mind_. It is also important to understand what is happening in the world today, which is why I suggest reading _The Cult of Trump_, which is essential for anyone wanting to understand the Trump phenomenon. These books will provide valuable insights and knowledge to help you navigate the complex world of cults and mind control.

CONCLUSION

At the beginning of this course, I shared the story of Laura, who was trapped in a Bible cult for 13 years and struggled with the mental health system for over a decade. I wanted to mention this story again to remind everyone that cult members are real people who have put their trust in us to help them. It's a significant responsibility, and we must take it seriously by being careful not to misdiagnose, seeking supervision and second opinions, and always listening to our clients. It is also crucial to track our client's progress in therapy to ensure that we provide effective and appropriate treatment. Finally, we must always remember that our clients' well-being and recovery depend on us, and we must do everything we can to help them.

Laura's story is a powerful reminder of the impact this work can have on people's lives. Helping individuals reclaim their power and live fulfilling lives is what drives me to do this work. I often get asked why I have been doing it for so many years, and my response is simple: it's the most rewarding thing I can do with my time. The feeling of helping someone realize they've been in a destructive cult and guiding them toward recovery is profound and inspiring. I am incredibly grateful for the opportunity to have worked with thousands of people and to now share my knowledge and experience through this course.

MODULE 9 RESOURCES

Freedom of Mind Resources

How to Rescue a Loved One from a Cult or Controlling Relationship: The Strategic Interactive Approach

Recovery from Spiritual Abuse and Healing Oneself to Trust Again

Strategic Interaction Approach (SIA) Frequently Asked Questions (FAQ)

Cult Deprogramming vs. Strategic Interactive Approach

Asperger's/ Autism Spectrum Disorder and Undue Influence

Autism, Extremism, And Protecting The Vulnerable With Dr. Tony Attwood

Invisible Storm: A Soldier's Memoir of Politics and PTSD by Jason Kander

Use of Words, Loaded Language, and "Thought Control" of Believers

Child-Centered Adoption: A Conversation with Dr. Joyce Maguire Pavao

Dismantling QAnon: A TEDxMidAtlantic Must Watch Program

Steven Hassan Dissertation: The BITE Model of Authoritarian Control

Videos

Karen Pressley, Ex-Scientologist, Paul Grosswald, and Steven Hassan talk

What is the Strategic Interactive Approach?

The Freedom of Mind Approach to Helping Individuals Born in High-Demand Groups and Cults

Books

Life Is in the Transitions: Mastering Change at Any Age by Bruce Feiler

The author explores the nature of life transitions, offering insights and strategies for navigating significant changes at various stages of life.

The Brain That Changes Itself: Stories of Personal Triumph from the Frontiers of Brain Science by Norman Doidge

This book presents groundbreaking discoveries in neuroscience, illustrating the brain's remarkable ability to change and adapt through neuroplasticity.

A History of God: The 4,000-Year Quest of Judaism, Christianity, and Islam by Karen Armstrong

The author traces the evolution of the concept of God in the three major monotheistic religions, revealing how beliefs have transformed over millennia.

Think Again: The Power of Knowing What You Don't Know by Adam Grant

This work encourages readers to embrace the art of rethinking and challenging one's own beliefs and assumptions to foster learning and growth.

From Dean's List to Dumpsters: Why I Left Harvard to Join a Cult by Jim Guerra

The memoir details the author's unexpected journey from academic excellence to life in a cult, highlighting the psychological factors that influence such drastic life choices.

ABOUT THE AUTHOR

Steven Hassan, PhD is a licensed mental health professional, a recognized expert on cults and undue influence, and possesses professional experience both in the United States and abroad.

His work encompasses various areas, including consultation, coaching, public speaking, media appearances, activism, writing, research, teaching, intervention, and recovery services, as well as expert consulting and testimony to aid individuals and families dealing with issues related to undue influence. Dr. Hassan also hosts *Cult Conversations: The Influence Continuum*, a podcast where he explores multiple different topics related to both cults, and various forms of both undue and positive influence.

Dr. Hassan's expertise extends to the realm of undue influence in a wide array of contexts, including destructive one-on-one relationships, family dynamics, parental alienation, small cult-like groups, religious cults, therapy and self-improvement groups, professional abuse, institutional abuse, corporate settings, multi-level marketing, political groups, human trafficking, colonialism, hate and violent extremism, and other challenging situations.

Throughout his 48 plus year career, Dr. Hassan has assisted countless individuals and families in recovering from undue influence as one of the world's foremost authorities on the subject of undue influence by both controlling groups and individuals. He possesses a unique perspective after his successful deprogramming in 1976 from the Moon cult. As a clinical professional, he has dedicated his life to sharing his vast experience to train and help people in need.

Additional work by Dr. Hassan and further resources may be found at freedomofmind. com.

www.ingramcontent.com/pod-product-compliance
Lightning Source LLC
Chambersburg PA
CBHW080248030426
42334CB00023BA/2739